The Wood-Carver of Salem

PLATE I.—Profile Medallion of Washington, hand carved in Wood, 1802.

The Wood-Carver of Salem

Samuel McIntire
His Life and Work

By

Frank Cousins and Phil M. Riley

Illustrated

AMS PRESS, INC.

NEW YORK

105349

Reprinted from the edition of 1916, Boston
First AMS EDITION published 1970
Manufactured in the United States of America

International Standard Book Number: 0-404-01786-X

Library of Congress Catalog Card Number: 74-119649

AMS PRESS, INC.
NEW YORK, N.Y. 10003

Foreword

ABOUT thirty years ago Mr. T. Frank Hunt, of Salem, suggested to Mr. Cousins that he undertake the task of making a comprehensive photographic record of the fine old houses of Salem, many of which could not be expected to exist permanently. All his life Mr. Cousins had been keenly appreciative of the remarkable history and splendid architecture of his native city; the idea appealed to him strongly and with the further commendation of Mr. John Robinson, of Peabody Museum, he finally decided to adopt it. From the outset both of these gentlemen were generous in valuable suggestions and material assistance in connection with the research necessary to bring to light a great amount of interesting historical data long buried in the quaint records of the Essex Institute, the City Hall of Salem, the Registry of Probate of Essex

County, and many old books, magazines, and newspapers.

In 1895 the architectural summer school of the Massachusetts Institute of Technology, held in Salem, impressed upon Mr. Cousins as never before the artistic and practical value of old Salem buildings, particularly the delightfully proportioned and admirably executed designs of Samuel McIntire, that master craftsman of the third period of Colonial architecture, and thus emphasized emphatically the true importance of his ambitious project. Ten years later, having accumulated over two thousand photographic negatives, he began to show the results of his labor to leading architects in the principal cities, fully a thousand of whom soon became his clients. This immediate recognition presently became even more gratifying by reason of the growing interest manifested in McIntire the man and his work, which culminated in a genuine demand for a book devoted to both. Among those to whom grateful acknowledgement is due for encouragement and inspiration in its preparation are: Mr. Louis C. Newhall, of Boston; Mr. Cass Gilbert and Mr. Electus D. Litchfield, of New York; Mr. Edward Robinson, Director of the Metropolitan Museum of Art, of New York; and

Foreword

Mr. Edward R. Smith, of Avery Library, Columbia University.

Five years ago Mr. Cousins was invited to meet the editors of *Country Life in America* and show them his photographs. At that time Mr. Riley was Architectural Editor, and the suggestion to write the text of a book devoted to the life and work of Samuel McIntire readily won his enthusiastic approval and enlisted his constructive support. He came to Salem to examine into the matter at first hand and after considerable investigation conceived the title and prepared the synopsis of "The Woodcarver of Salem." Then followed much painstaking joint effort; the book commenced to take tangible form, and a sincere attempt was made to phrase a true estimate of McIntire's achievements, and by impartial criticism to interpret in a logical and entertaining manner its value and significance in modern home building. Thus this volume represents a real collaboration the perusal of which, it is hoped, may prove as informative and pleasurable to the reader as its preparation has been to the authors.

FRANK COUSINS AND PHIL M. RILEY.

SEPTEMBER 15, 1916.

Contents

List of Plates

[xi]

List of Plates

List of Plates

[xiii]

List of Plates

List of Plates

[xv]

List of Plates

List of Plates

[xvii]

List of Plates

List of Plates

List of Plates

The Wood-Carver of Salem

The Wood-Carver of Salem

CHAPTER I

SALEM ARCHITECTURE

FEW cities in the United States can boast a residential section, still well preserved and occupied by the best families, which suggests only the long-distant past with virtually no intrusive indication of modernity to mar the illusion. Salem, Massachusetts, is among the foremost. That its beauties have been so abundantly preserved to posterity seems to be almost a miracle — particularly when one recalls the great conflagration of 1914 — and miracles are always happy. One may also marvel at the remarkably perfect condition of the woodwork on these old houses as it exists in Salem to-day, proving conclusively that for white-painted exterior wood trim no wood, unless it be cypress, excels white pine for endurance. Street after street in this remarkable city, so rich in historic lore, is lined with houses to which intelligent citizens point with pride because of their pristine beauty, their age, and the splendid manner in which they have been maintained, in many instances for considerably more than a century. Here, indeed, is an example of true New England spirit and Yankee thrift.

Amid such surroundings fancy readily transports the imaginative mind back to the days when Washington, La Fayette, and other men distinguished in the early affairs of the nation were guests within these very-welcoming doorways. In fact, to wander about among the old houses and gardens of Salem is to see a vivid reflection of that golden age when this fascinating place was counted among the principal centers of culture and wealth; when leaders in art, science, and letters were familiar figures in the streets, and when prosperous merchants and eminent statesmen called the town "home."

Next to Plymouth the oldest settlement in Massachusetts, Salem quickly attained civic and commercial importance because of its early origin and seacoast situation; the people, too, were of high ideals, sincere determination, and steadfast purpose — the sort that achieve greatness. Theirs was the first armed resistance to British tyranny at the North Bridge two months before Paul Revere's immortal ride, and during the Revolution it was their privateers, carrying upward of two thousand guns, which took four hundred and forty-five prizes — more than were taken by the ships of all the other ports combined. The entire merchant marine became engaged in privateering, and new ships were built as rapidly as possible, until the number flying Salem signals at the close of the Revolution was said to have been one hundred and fifty-eight. By far the greater portion of the male population of the town was engaged either in building ships or in a seafaring life. Shipbuilding became a fine art, so to speak; Salem vessels could outsail almost anything then afloat, and their cabins were the supreme achievement of skilled joiners and wood-carvers, attracted thither by this industry from all sections of the country.

In later, happier days, these very ships, and others built in the quarter century that followed, made Salem the center of commerce and refinement that it became. An idle fleet, more ably manned than any before it, had to be peacefully employed. With admirable courage and remarkable foresight, its owners entered into business relations with the East Indies and other far ports of the world never before reached by trading ships, and thus Salem became our chief port of entry long before New York, Boston, and Philadelphia were even known to the merchants of the East. In 1807 Salem had 252 vessels, aggregating 43,570 tons. These ventures brought great wealth to shipowners and captains with which to build more pretentious homes than had previously supplied their somewhat frugal necessities. During the thirty years prior to 1811, Salem merchants paid into the Custom-house in duties more than eleven million dollars, which gives an indication of the tremendous amount of their business. The refining influence of their extensive foreign travels demanded a better standard of living, and the rare furniture, wall papers, and other objects of art which they had collected called for appropriate home surroundings in which to display them. This provided a higher type of employment for the more versatile of their shipbuilders, and the intelligence and native ingenuity with which these craftsmen adapted the motives of the Renaissance to their own radically different problems is truly remarkable.

That was during the optimistic days a hundred years ago; but the wheel of progress has turned, as turn it will, and Salem now lives chiefly in the glory of its illustrious past, reminders of which are to be seen in nearly every one of the principal streets.

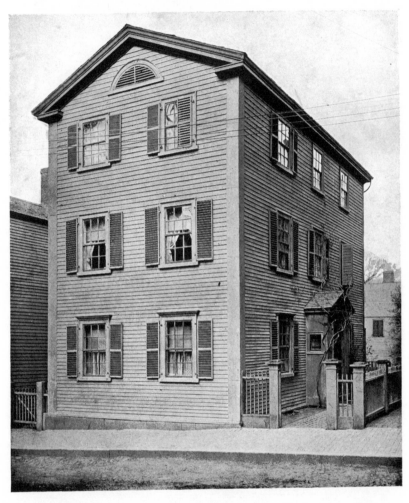

PLATE II.—The Home of Samuel McIntire, 31 Summer Street, Salem, Mass.

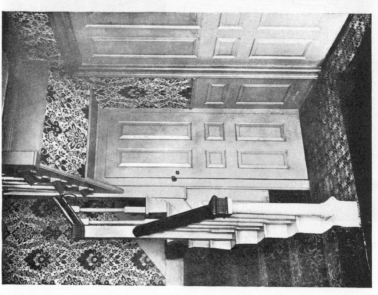

Plate III.—The Lower and Upper Halls of McIntire's Home.

Salem Architecture

No longer does the ring of the hammer resound in the shipyard of the Beckets; no longer are rich cargoes from all the great ports of the world discharged at Derby and Crowninshield wharves; no longer do anxious merchants scan the horizon to seaward from the belvederes and cupolas of their beautiful homes. Salem is no longer mistress of the seas; her splendid merchant marine, said to comprise one hundred and ninety-eight ships in 1825, gradually began to decrease in number upon the coming of the railroads, which built up the ports of large cities at the expense of smaller towns. The foreign commerce of Salem is a thing of the past, but most of the homes of her former distinguished men stand intact to-day, compelling universal admiration for their refined, substantial beauty, and comprising in many respects the most notable collection of early American architecture.

In terms of the so-called Colonial style, our national heritage, Salem is the architectural center of New England, and to New England and Virginia must be accorded the highest places in our regard as the principal fountains of our culture and development. But the architecture of Virginia implies the great estate; it is neither for the town nor the masses. Thus it is that in Salem oftener than elsewhere leading architects and discriminating home builders have found inspiration for modern adaptation. One ever goes to Salem as to a great storehouse of American antiquities, walking along her principal streets in admiration and entering her historic homes with reverence. Indeed, this fascinating historic city has become a synonym for the best in Colonial architecture, notably doorways and chimney pieces. Variety and the opportunity for comparison render Salem architecture unique and especially valuable in that it embraces three dissimilar types — one might say four, since they were developed in four distinct periods. First came the lean-to, the average date of the examples still standing being about that of the witchcraft delusion of 1692; next followed the gambrel-roof type about 1750; then came the three-story, square wooden house of 1785, and finally the three-story, square brick construction of 1818. None of these aspires to the manorial splendor of the South, but each frankly interprets the refinement, the domestic spirit, and reasonable degree of dignity of the people, quite as true in the prosperous period of brick construction as in the earlier years, when the snug comfort of the lean-to sufficed.

Strictly speaking, the first two periods constitute the only really Colonial houses in Salem, but the

custom everywhere is to place in the Colonial cate-
gory all houses with classic detail up to the beginning
of the so-called Greek revival about 1825, when the
vogue came to give houses of wood as nearly as possible the form and aspect of the Doric temple in its
purest and severest form. This is logical and proper,
inasmuch as the mansions immediately preceding
and following the Revolution were a direct development of their simpler predecessors and hence very
closely related to them. Such a broad application
of the word seems particularly happy in connection
with Salem architecture which did not attain the
full measure of its development until after the Revolution.

The word "Provincial" has been suggested as a
more accurate substitute for Colonial, the argument
being that little worthy of serious architectural consideration was erected in America during the actual
Colonial period. On this basis those splendid houses
built during the first three or four decades of our
national life should no doubt be termed "Federal."
But, after all, the word matters little in comparison
with its meaning, provided the latter be well under-
stood. The name Colonial has taken the popular
fancy and become a byword on every lip, while the
architecture it designates, principally because of its

very comprehensiveness, expresses our national spirit as nearly as we have been able to express it.

In those days of maritime prosperity large families were the rule, not the exception, and the very number of rooms required, when a state of affluence made large ones possible, tended toward a square house. And it was in this square Colonial town house that Salem architecture reached the pinnacle of its achievement. Although eloquent in substantial comfort and dignified appearance, it had not the picturesque appeal of the lean-to or the gambrel-roof types, yet in its ornamental detail it far surpassed them both. Severe, almost ugly in line and mass, such a structure needed considerable embellishment in order to ensure an attractive appearance. Quickened by this obvious requirement and the spirit of the time, which ever called for more elaborate externals corresponding to the great wealth being amassed in foreign trade, local builders turned more frequently for inspiration to the published works of the master architects of the Renaissance. The classic orders were modified to domestic uses and applied throughout; both exterior and interior features responded to the influence. The hard outlines of the structure as a whole, and especially the plainness of flat-boarded façades, were relieved by imposing pilaster treatments; flat roofs were decked with balustrades, and hip roofs terminated in ornamental cupolas or balustraded belvederes; columned and pedimented porches shielded the doorways; architrave casings of doors and windows, both inside and outside, were elaborated by completing the entablature with cornice and frieze to form an ornamental head; cornices with elegant hand-tooled moldings and often supported by modillions were placed under overhanging eaves and at the ceiling of interiors.

In the execution of this work, Salem architects and builders were quick to call to their aid the more accomplished of the wood-carvers employed in the local shipyards, then the largest in America. The previous training of these craftsmen and their skill in the use of sharp-edged tools made it an easy matter for them to adapt to their needs and execute in wood the moldings and other classic detail which their fellow workers across the sea were cutting in stone. Done in a masterly manner indicating intelligent study as well as clever adaptation, the work in its translation to wood took on a lightness and grace which has come to be regarded as one of the principal charms of the Colonial work in this locality. Considering the crude tools of those days, one's admiration for the nicety with which the fine-scale detail was cut need know no bounds, for it compares favorably with the finest handiwork of our most painstaking workmen of to-day. Even simple moldings had to be made with hand planes, while those bearing further enrichment were of necessity carved laboriously with gouges and other chisels.

In the free atmosphere of a new country virtually without local tradition, untrammeled by the letter of European precedent, and immediately influenced by the fanciful rope moldings and other flamboyant decorations then being prepared all about them for ship cabins, these wood-carvers and joiners succeeded in imparting to their work a delightful spontaneity and particular fitness ; it possesses distinguishing traits peculiar to itself. Even the neighboring towns do not anywhere, in work of the same period, disclose several of the more distinctive motives of Salem's resourceful craftsmen. In admirable proportions her architecture is more highly refined; in exceptional precision of workmanship more uniform ; in decorative detail more delicate and chaste. But, above all else, it commands favorable attention for its frequent unconventionality and even novelty, combined with marked restraint and undeniable good taste. Not only did the Salem architects in-

PLATE IV.—Detail of Mantel in the Front Chamber of McIntire's Home; Detail of Mantel in the Chamber where McIntire died.

PLATE V.—Detail of a Door in McIntire's Home; Mantel and Cornice in the Front Chamber.

terpret the orders with considerable freedom, vary-
ing the moldings, rearranging their relation one to
another, and altering proportions for variety of effect, but they neither hesitated to combine moldings from two orders in one entablature nor to
substitute for any of them clever innovations of their
own, which usually preserved virtually the same
scale.   Cornice and frieze were often utilized without
the architrave, but it was chiefly in the bed-molding
or dentil course underneath the corona of the cornice,
whether outdoors or inside and however employed,
that the more prominent alterations were made.
In its resourceful initiative, the work of these men
is more nearly creative and hence less interpretive
than that of the early craftsmen of any other locality. Not subservient to the classic orders as
evolved by the ancients, nor yet as modified by the
leaders of the Renaissance, they dominated them,
cleverly molding them anew to meet their own radically different needs, with the result that their work
became more intimately an expression of its creators
than did the Georgian in England.

These old mansions of Salem, representing the
very flower of a remarkable architectural period,
bespeak the earnest study of every prospective home
builder.   A visit to this quaintly picturesque city

invariably moves the most blasé student of architecture to eloquence, yet to extol its praises amounts only to humming the chorus of the song. Whether one go to Salem or to one of the several other early American centers of wealth and culture for local color, it should not be forgotten that the principal theme is the Colonial style, now more securely rooted in popular esteem than ever before and more frequently influencing the character of the houses now being erected than any other guiding spirit. This happy outcome finds a more lively appreciation in that it corrects an aberration in the logical development of our building traditions.

It will be recalled that for half a century after the advent of the Greek revival, the Colonial style completely lost its power of appeal. Fads and fancies took the country by storm, but as the processes of our economic and social evolution ever turned our eyes backward to scrutinize the fundamentals of our national life in the solution of the more complex problems of passing years, so the attempt to lift American architecture out of that slough of despond known as the Victorian period led architects back surely and directly to the supreme achievements of our early craftsmen, there to resume the perpetuation of a heritage as fine as that of any country, unless it be Greece itself. It was inevitable that the Colonial tradition should persist, but this was due as much to the development of a higher average mentality as to the efforts of architects, though they were naturally the leaders. Whereas just prior to the dawn of the present century the pioneers among them were accorded scant encouragement in their efforts to revive and adapt this architecture of a bygone day, its advocacy now meets with genuine enthusiasm in most quarters. The whole people seems to respond to the magic word Colonial, and, stirred by a keener consciousness of the meaning of our nationality and quickened by a growing appreciation of its founders and early supporters, is finding a wholesome and appealing significance in the architecture of those brave days and likewise a prototype decidedly worthy of emulation. The dissensions engendered by the Civil War, also the unfortunate architectural delusions of that period, have been forgotten. We are now a people more strongly united than ever before in our history, and in architecture we have finally bridged the gap of intervening years and begun, as in all things else, to build for the future as well as the present upon the fundamentals of the past. In such measure do we accord to architecture a continuity

as certain as that of the other fine arts in America,
and by a rational, concerted national viewpoint do
we lay the foundation for a strong and clearly defined
American style; a living style, ever sufficiently
related to the past yet always susceptible of greater
refinement and further adaptation to the spirit and
needs of each successive generation; a style that
though old is yet ever new ; a style to which distinguishing local traits may be imparted; a style that
lends itself to public and commercial as well as
domestic uses.

Thus it may truthfully be said that the real
American style now is, always has been, and probably always will be Colonial. Inseparably wrapped
up in our glorious history, it has become a conspicuous expression of our national life. Its delightful
grace, repose, and dignity never fail to make direct
appeal to every thinking person possessed of a keen
sense of good design and proportion or a ready appreciation of our early traditions. In Colonial,
rather than the styles brought from far afield, does one
find complete fitness, absolute sincerity, and sheer
beauty. Embracing the varied Renaissance expressions of the Dutch and French as well as the
English peoples in America, it evolved among us the
one distinctive type of American architecture which

has aroused the admiration of the world; it is ours, and we cherish it.

Of course the intrinsic merit which is perpetuating the Colonial style lies in its complete suitability and ready adaptability to new uses and present-day requirements, for happily they are becoming oftener the dictates of comfort than of ostentatious appearance, although Colonial motives possess that rare quality of seeming appropriate for either a mansion or a cottage when sympathetically interpreted. Indeed, it daily arouses our admiration anew, solving our ever more complex building problems gracefully and well when other styles fail, and ensuring a home of which the owner will not tire during a lifetime, and which his descendants will be proud to inherit.

The occasional criticism that the style is somewhat restricted in its possibilities loses force when one considers not the examples in Salem or any one locality alone but the entire manifestation both in the North and the South. Surely no dearth of evidence exists to the effect that Colonial is varied enough for our purposes. Found from Maine to Louisiana, and differing considerably in the several localities, according to size, climatic conditions, constructive materials, and other personal influences, it appeals to us more strongly than any style derived from other sources. How similar yet how different are the New England lean-to, the square Salem town house, the gambrel-roof cottage of the Dutch middle colonies, the hooded, gable-roof Pennsylvania farmhouse, and the stately, porticoed plantation mansion of the South. Despite the similarity and relatively small number of motives, how varied are the effects of altered detail, scale, and arrangement as applied to structures of differing outline, mass, and constructive material. The marked absence of monotony in Salem, for instance, where everything of consequence is Colonial, indicates beyond question that any occurrence of monotonous similarity in neighboring houses must ever be ascribed to the unresourcefulness of the architect rather than to a restricted medium of expression. In fact, whatever one's preference as to local color, and whether one go to Salem or elsewhere for the scale and proportion of the detail, this much is certain, that those basic motives from which the Colonial style springs live as surely to-day as they did over a century ago, and, thanks to the wisdom of our foremost architects, will continue to live in the hearts, the minds, and the sight of true Americans.

PLATE VI.—McIntire's Gravestone, Charter Street Burial Ground.

PLATE VII.—Petition for a Public Pump signed by McIntire; McIntire's Autograph on the Petition.

CHAPTER II

SAMUEL AND THE OTHER McINTIRES

OF the many Salem craftsmen in wood, most of them long since forgotten, one family of wood-carvers, joiners, and housewrights, named McIntire, whose skill descended through several generations, stands forth conspicuously because of a genius among them named Samuel. The son of Joseph and Sarah (Ruck) McIntire, Samuel was born January 16, 1757, in the gambrel-roof house at the corner of Mill and Norman Streets, Salem, now considerably remodeled and numbered 2 and 4 Mill Street. This house had been built by his father, himself a housewright, so that Samuel was born and came to man's estate in the atmosphere of his father's work. In his father's shop he learned the trade of carpenter and joiner and, as the result of persevering application with his tools and of cultivating his inherent sense of design through persistent study of the classic masters, he became probably the most highly skilled American wood-carver of his time.

These were exciting years in our national history and that through their influence McIntire became ardently patriotic and a staunch supporter of those fine principles of liberty, of justice, and of humanity, to which we as a people have been devoted from the first, is indicated by the impulse which prompted him to excel in carving that symbol of American ideals, the eagle, and to exalt the national consciousness as well as to exhibit his own loyalty by its frequent use in a variety of ways wherever consistent with the work in hand.

Spurred by the hearty praise and constant encouragement of Rev. William Bentley, historian and pastor of the East Church, McIntire was finally induced to carry his carving to the point of assaying his skill in the field of sculpture in its true sense. His several modest achievements in this direction showed great promise, and had he lived this versatile man would doubtless have won renown in this department of the fine arts also. His bust of Governor Winthrop, carved in wood in 1789 for Doctor Bentley, and now in the possession of the American Antiquarian Society, is no mean achievement, and the complete ornamental figure of a reaper, surmounting the roof of the summerhouse formerly on the Elias Haskett Derby farm in Danvers, compares favorably with most similar work in plaster or marble. Referring to the sculptors who at various periods have made enviable names for themselves in Salem, Felt in his "Annals of Salem" writes:

"Among our later sculptors, Samuel McIntire was noted. He died 1811, aged 54. So was his brother Joseph, who deceased June 11, 1825. The son of the latter, who still survives (1849), has exhibited a similar genius."

The education of Samuel McIntire's boyhood was meager and did not exceed that of his fellows, but, like others whom the world has heard from, this did not deter him. Realizing that the ability to read opens all doors to a determined mind, the thirst for knowledge led him to spend much of what he could earn for books that he might familiarize himself as nearly as possible with some of those things which his lack of a college education and his inability to travel had denied him. With few exceptions these dearly bought volumes were devoted to the fine arts, and he made the most of them, studying every page repeatedly with increasing comprehension, making their precepts his ideals, and translating them into terms of his own craftsmanship.

[19]

In 1777 his father died intestate, and Samuel, for a consideration, released all rights to his father's property, which was apportioned among his mother, Sarah (Ruck) McIntire, his two aunts, Deborah and Mahitable McIntire, and his brothers Joseph and Angier. Joseph succeeded to the business of his father, and the following year, August 31, 1778, Samuel married Elizabeth Field, the ceremony being performed by Rev. Thomas Barnard, pastor of the North Church and the hero of the North Bridge incident referred to elsewhere. Quickened by the loving encouragement of a congenial helpmate, his meteoric career then began in very earnest, first as a carver, then as a designer, and finally as an architect. In 1782 we find him the architect of the Pierce-Johonnot-Nichols house, one of his greatest works, and from that time until his death, nearly thirty years later, according to Rev. William Bentley, he dominated the architecture of Salem. That he could have reached this third and ultimate stage of his career within five years from the inception of his independent enterprise and at the age of twenty-five speaks eloquently of the thorough training of his father as well as of his own aptitude, determination, and energy.

But those were ambitious days for the youth of Salem; the wonderful exploits of her more adven-

turous sons at sea set a pace which those at home
could match only by the utmost of persistent en-
deavor. When one recalls that Benjamin W. Crowninshield, who finally became Secretary of the Navy,
and his three brothers each sailed his own ship at
the age of twenty, one begins to comprehend the
spirit of do and dare which developed at home the
statesmen, jurists, writers, educators, architects,
painters, sculptors, and musicians, who, with her
merchants and sea captains, won for Salem the renown and unique place she has always occupied in
the annals of New England and of the nation.

Once established in his career, McIntire bought the
modest, three-story, gable-roof house at Number 31
Summer Street which had been built in 1780 and there
he lived until his death. He was too busy with the
commissions of others to build for himself such a
home as he might have liked, and no record or tradition tells whether he improved this house to any
considerable extent. The charming mantels resemble his work, and the stairway, doors, and other
wood finish, although of the utmost simplicity,
possess a certain quaint distinction that pleases
the eye; had it been otherwise they would doubtless have offended his sensitive taste and been replaced. The front of the third story was McIntire's

music room, its coved ceiling under the roof probably being his own idea. Here he had his organ and other musical instruments, and that it was the best room of the house and the place where he entertained his friends is shown by the inventory of his effects at the time of his death which appraises the chairs at a higher value than those of the parlor on the first floor.

In the rear of his house stood the shop where most of the wood finish and exquisite carving for McIntire's houses were prepared.   About 1840 this building was moved to Tapleyville, Danvers, and built into a dwelling there.

A third dwelling still standing in Salem is of much interest in connection with the life of McIntire. Then the home of Samuel Field, it was in the house at Number 90 Washington Street that McIntire courted and married Field's daughter Elizabeth. The records show that for about five years, from 1785 to 1790, McIntire held a mortgage on the front half of this house. The lower front room was then occupied as an insurance office, and here McIntire probably transacted much of his business, for an insurance company in those days was an association of merchants, and his frequent presence there brought him in touch with the leading men of Salem,

PLATE VIII.—Summer House formerly on Elias Haskett Derby's
Peabody Farm.

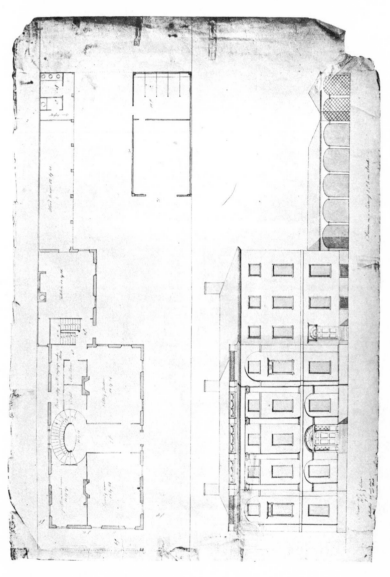

PLATE IX.—McIntire's Plans of an unknown End-to-the-Street House.

by whom he was employed. With the construction of the Courthouse near by and his other residential work, McIntire was exceedingly busy during that period and much in need of an office near the center of the town's business section. Elias Haskett Derby then lived at Number 70 Washington Street, only two estates north on the same side, and with thoughts of his future mansion maturing in his mind, was probably watching McIntire's development with interest. Derby's patronage continued throughout his life and meant much to McIntire even after Derby's death, for the Derbys, Crowninshields, Peabodys, Wests, and other prominent families were closely related by marriage and inclined to follow the lead of the senior Derby.

That every rung in McIntire's remarkable ladder of achievement was sound and represented the direct result of real merit and genuine progress can be shown readily. It is generally conceded that the best carving of McIntire's time was done in Salem; contemporary critics so referred to it, as may be seen in many old books, magazines, and newspapers. Certainly nothing to excel it in quantity, quality, and variety has been found elsewhere, and thanks to the enduring character of white pine, these merits need not be taken as a matter of hearsay but may be corroborated by any appreciative person who will visit this quaint city. McIntire is the one name which has persisted to this day in connection with the best of this work, so it may be said with justice that he was probably the greatest American carver of his time. As evidenced by quotations which follow later in this chapter, he was so regarded by writers of that period. Even to-day his work needs no written encomiums; its delicacy and precision speak for themselves to every competent observer.

As a designer McIntire stood second to none in America. We find even our foremost designers of the present day and students of things Colonial sitting at the feet, as it were, of this master crafts-man of a century ago — this man of the chisel, the plane, and the saw — whose workroom was graced by no institutional diploma, yet who by his rare skill in the use of tools and his innate good taste demonstrated the beneficial influence of a sympa-thetic relation and intimate working knowledge be-tween artist and artisan. Obviously the man who can execute his own designs in a superlative manner becomes potentially the greater designer, and so with McIntire. He realized both the extent and limitations of his medium; likewise he appreciated the capabilities of his men and knew by actual ex-

perience the restrictions imposed by even the best
tools available in those days. And with this knowledge he had the clever common sense never to court
failure by attempting to exceed the confines of either.
While he demonstrated again and again his own personal ability to carve even at very fine scale with a
delicacy of execution equal to that of the best sculptors in clay, he himself could tool only a small frac-
tion of the decorative material required for the
hundred or so houses which were built or improved
under his direction during the thirty years of his
practice. The time and expense would have been
prohibitive, and he naturally welcomed the advent
of applied stucco, composition, or French putty prepared from casts or molds after the Adam manner
as a means to attain greater delicacy of detail and
precision of workmanship more quickly and at smaller
cost. When glued in place and painted, the applied
pieces could not be distinguished from the wood, so
that it combined well with the hand-planed and
carved moldings. Most of this applied work was imported from England, but several motives not to be
found in other than McIntire's houses so resemble
some of his carvings in wood as to lend color to the
conclusion that they may have been cast from designs or actual carvings by him. It is not unrea-

sonable to suppose that his creative ability stood him in good stead here as in working out new moldings, and certainly the detailed plan of carved moldings and applied work for the oval room of the Elias Haskett Derby mansion indicates that he gave close attention to the composition of this ornamental detail. That he so quickly grasped the possibilities of this new art and so intelligently made it part of his own work discloses a keen understanding of his trade and remarkable foresight as well, for this method has stood the test of time and to-day is more widely used than ever. In this, as in his hand-tooled work, it is the exceptionally pleasing proportions which have so strongly appealed to architects. A subtle balance is always maintained between plain surface and rich decoration, and as compared with other contemporary work in Salem and elsewhere his displays greater refinement of detail and a generally lighter and more graceful effect; always it was delicate without weakness and rich without ostentation.

Although at the outset McIntire executed most of his decorative woodwork himself, this became impossible as his practice broadened to include the functions of designer and architect, and he began to depend more and more upon the craftsmanship of his two brothers, Joseph, nine years his senior, and Angier, two years his junior, who were housewrights — that is carpenters and master builders, — his own son, Samuel F. McIntire, and his brother Joseph's son, Joseph, both of whom were accomplished carvers. The magnificent east parlor of the Pierce-Johonnot-Nichols house, best known and most admired of all his artistry, probably represents the work of all five McIntires, four craftsmen working under the direction of Samuel, the designer, architect, and master craftsmen of them all. The same is doubtless true of the Elias Haskett Derby mansion, the Tucker-Rice house, the Derby-Crown-inshield-Rogers house, and "Oak Hill." In none of these will be found anything conventionally classic as a whole. Greek and Roman detail was intelligently varied and recombined in a manner to elicit enthusiastic commendation for individuality in design, good taste, and resourcefulness in adaptation.

The tendency on the part of a few writers of the present day to deny to McIntire the full measure of credit due him for his achievements, to state, as some have done, that he was hardly an architect but merely a clever carver and builder, or to infer that he cannot be regarded as a great architect because of the trifling fact that all his houses were of

the three-story square type and built in the vicinity
of Salem, betokens no intent to do his memory in-
justice; rather it betrays a woeful ignorance of the
written records regarding the man and his accomplishments, of which there is a considerable number
in the literature of his day and the legal records of
Salem.

To say that he is our foremost Colonial architect
of domestic buildings is a strong statement indeed,
yet what other designer of this period did so much
work as well? To dispute that in this field
McIntire's eminence equals that of Bulfinch in
public buildings presents a task which one may
well hesitate to attempt. That few encyclopædias
and library catalogs even list his name and only
fugitive references are to be found in books of Colonial architecture belittles his work not at all. Unlike Bulfinch, who had a daughter to collect, preserve,
and publish most of the papers her father ever
touched pen to, McIntire had no one to herald
him upon his death, with the result that the facts
have become buried in the old records of Salem,
and no one has taken the time and trouble to dig
them out except a few antiquaries. Yet, despite
the oblivion into which his life had passed, the
beautiful, refined architecture of Salem and vicinity,

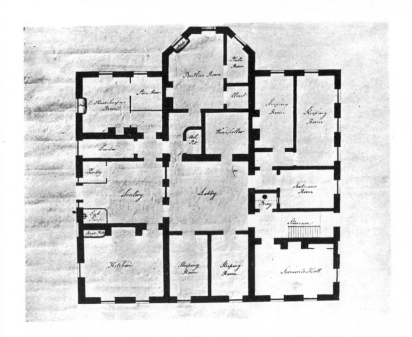

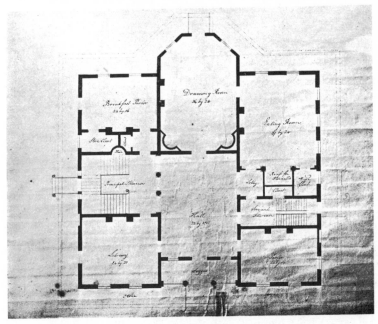

PLATE X.—Basement and Street Floor Plans of an unknown house
by McIntire.

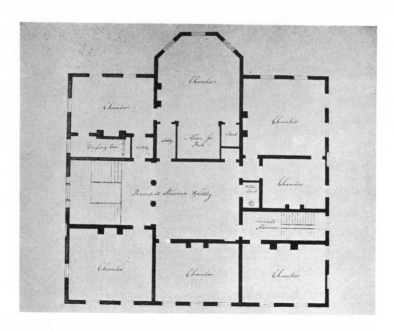

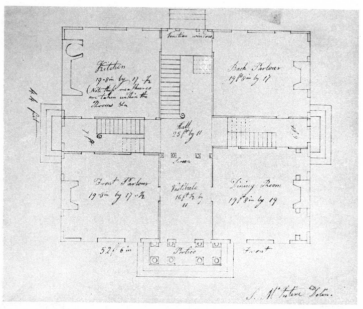

PLATE XI.—Chamber and Street Floor Plans of unknown
houses by McIntire.

as planned, designed, and hand-tooled by McIntire
with the assistance of his relatives, stands as an enduring monument which requires no written eulogy,
for it is known through the medium of photographs
to fully a thousand prominent architects in all parts
of the country who have admired, studied, and
adapted its splendid motives and superb detail to
their needs. His doorways, chimney pieces, and other
wood trim have furnished the inspiration for more
of the best modern Colonial houses than the work
of any other one man. Through this medium and
the appearance of a few recent magazine articles
by the authors and others, interested laymen are
also beginning to know and appreciate McIntire's
genius so that a permanent record of his name in
the honored place it deserves in the early history of
American architecture now seems assured.

McIntire's exceptional ability as an architect
cannot be questioned when Rev. William Bentley's
diary, McIntire's gravestone, and the obituary notices in *The Essex Register* and *The Salem Gazette*,
all quoted later in this chapter, refer to McIntire's
talents as an architect. The Historical Collection
of the Essex Institute has references to his work as
an architect far too numerous to quote, and those
who will take the trouble to examine the records at

City Hall will find that Joseph Cloutman, town clerk, made the following entry:

> *Age 54 Mr. Samuel McIntire, carver*
> *" The Architect of Salem "*

Bentley wrote in his diary that upon the death of McIntire, "no man is left to be consulted upon a new plan of execution beyond his bare practice", and in corroboration of this, Bulfinch designed the Essex Bank, now the house of The Salem Fraternity, in 1811, and the Almshouse in 1816. The former, the oldest boys' club in the country, was organized in 1869 to provide evening instruction and wholesome amusement for those who "being confined to their work during the day need recreation at the end of their labors." In addition to physical training and general education, there are classes devoted to many of the principal arts and crafts, a well filled library and reading room. One cannot but think what such privileges would have meant to McIntire had they existed during his boyhood.

These two buildings, the only ones designed by Bulfinch in Salem, emphasize the loss McIntire's death meant to the community. Indeed, it may rightly be regarded as a significant fact that the creative influence of the McIntire family upon the architecture of Salem ended with the death of McIntire's son, Samuel F., in 1819, and that nothing of note belonging to this period was built after 1818. Felt's "Annals of Salem" and *The Massachusetts Magazine* for March, 1790, both contain the statement that McIntire was the architect of the Courthouse of 1785, his plans being executed by Daniel Bancroft. Rev. C. C. Beaman writes in the Historical Collection of the Essex Institute that McIntire was the architect of the Branch Meeting House and named the seven master carpenters who executed separate parts of the work on contract. In an old letter Perley Putnam states that the Nathan Read house was designed by Samuel McIntire and built by his brother Joseph and other carpenters.

McIntire's plans preserved at the Essex Institute, and those of the proposed national capitol in the possession of the Maryland Historical Society, many of them signed and all bearing hand-writing easily identified as his, also indicate his activities as an architect. Although upon comparison with modern building plans McIntire's draftsmanship may seem crude and his small-scale floor plans and simple elevations, devoted chiefly to mass, fenestration, and the principal doorway, cornice, balustrade, and other ornament may appear somewhat incomplete, it must be remembered that the architect's calling had not then become the highly specialized profession it now is. Every architect was then primarily a craftsman, a carver, a joiner, or housewright as well as a designer, and often himself the man to execute the designs, and was thus less in need of details carefully laid out to scale; always the work was done under the direct supervision of the architect.

Being primarily a carver, McIntire left the erection of the structure itself to such successful housewrights as his brothers, Joseph and Angier, and devoted himself chiefly to the design and preparation of the wood trim and other ornamental features which were made in his own shop by skilled carvers and joiners, among whom his son, Samuel F., and his nephew, Joseph, finally took the lead, often revealing skill almost equal to his own. There is no evidence that Samuel McIntire was a builder or contractor in the modern sense; but he was virtually an architect in the modern sense and a designer and and carver of note as well. His work as an architect calls for no apology; neither can his claim to greatness be denied because his houses were all of the square type. In this he was following the tendency of the time throughout New England, and what the type lacked in picturesqueness of line and mass he supplied in variety of embellishment as seen in his doorways, porches, windows, cornices, roofs, and occasional pilaster treatment of the façade. The adoption of brick in his later work considerably broadened its scope, and he demonstrated also that variety can be obtained even in the so-called square house by variation of the floor plan, sometimes actually square, as in the Pierce-Johonnot-Nichols house, again rectangular and broadside to the street, as in the Clifford Crowinshield house, or rectangular and end to the street, as in the Josiah Dow house. In this latter instance the ell and outbuildings adjoin the end of the main house and elongate the rectangular arrangement, whereas in the Gardner-White-Pingree house, for instance, which stands broadside to the street, they adjoin the broad rear side.

McIntire proved his versatility by his public work, to which the last chapter of this volume is devoted. True, his activities in this as well as in the domestic field were confined to Salem and its vicinity, and therein lies much to his credit. To be so highly appreciated at home in itself meant much; he found all he could reasonably attempt to do in Salem, and as it was then our greatest port of entry and in every way important as a civic center, why need he look elsewhere? So far as is known, his competitive plan for the national capitol at Washington was his only attempt to do so. Other unsuccessful competing architects were Benjamin Henry Latrobe and Charles Bulfinch who in turn supervised the building of the capitol as designed and begun by Doctor William Thornton, and it is fair to presume that had he lived McIntire also would eventually have had an active part in its completion and enlargement.

While, as already stated, there appears to be no definite proof of McIntire's having designed any house or other building beyond the confines of the old township of Salem, one occasionally sees noble structures in New England seaport towns that must have been his work or inspired by it. The best builders came to Salem from all parts of Massachusetts and New Hampshire to seek inspiration, and many of the less versatile did not hesitate to copy his detail outright. As an instance in point, the visitor to Portsmouth, New Hampshire, will find in Middle Street a large, square house with a pilaster treatment of the façade so like that of the Derby-Crowninshield-Rogers house in Salem as at least to suggest McIntire influence.

PLATE XII.—Window Head from Elias Haskett Derby Mansion, and other woodwork preserved at the Essex Institute.

PLATE XIII.—Detail of Fence and Ornamental Post, 25 Chestnut Street; Stone Gatepost, Charles Street Entrance to Boston Public Garden, adapted from McIntire's earlier wood design.

Samuel and the other McIntires

One likes to look into the face of such a man and read his character as his life has written it there, but unfortunately no painting or other portrait of McIntire is known to exist. The most illuminating picture of him is found in the written words of his warm friend, wise counselor, and stanch advocate, Rev. William Bentley, pastor of the East Church, Salem, who, on February 7, 1811, the day after McIntire's death, wrote in his diary as follows:

"This day Salem is deprived of one of the most ingenious men it had in it. Samuel McIntire, aet. 54, in Summer street. He was descended of a family of Carpenters who had no claims on public favor and was educated at a branch of that business. By attention he soon gained a superiority to all of his occupation and the present Court House, the North and South Meeting houses, and indeed all the improvements of Salem for nearly thirty years past have been under his eye. In Sculpture he had no rival in New England and I possess some specimens which I should not scruple to compare with any I ever saw. To the best of my abilities I encouraged him in this branch. In music he had a good taste and tho' not presuming to be an original composer, he was among our best Judges and most able performers. All the instruments we use he could understand and was the best person to be employed in correcting any defects, or repairing them. He had a fine person, a majestic appearance, calm countenance, great self command and amiable temper. He was welcome but never intruded. He had complained of some obstruction in the chest, but when he died it was unexpectedly. The late increase of workmen in wood has been from the demand for exportation and this has added nothing to the character and reputation of the workman, so that upon the death of Mr. McIntire no man is left to be consulted upon a new plan of execution beyond his bare practice."

The following day, February 8, 1811, a notice of his death appeared in *The Salem Gazette* which indicated the high esteem in which McIntire was held by the community at large:

"In this town, Mr. Samuel M'Intire, carver, age 54 years — a man very much beloved and sincerely lamented. His funeral will be from his late dwelling house in Summer Street, at 3 o'clock Saturday afternoon, where his relations and friends are requested to attend.

"We have received a just and respectful tribute, from one who knew him well, to the genius and virtues of the deceased and lamented Mr. M'Intire.

We regret that it comes too late for insertion this day, but we shall most cordially give it place in our next."

In similar vein, the following appeared in *The Essex Register* of February 9, 1811:

"In this town, Mr. Samuel M'Intire, aged 54. His talents in architecture, sculpture and music were distinguished. His manners combined suavity, purity and firm character. His industry, usefulness and consistent virtues gave him an uncommon share of the affections of all who knew him. By his own well directed energies he became one of the best of men. His funeral will be from his late dwelling house in Summer Street at 3 o'clock on Monday afternoon, if fair weather. If not the next fair day, which his friends and relatives are requested to attend."

On February 12, 1811 the promised "tribute", written by a very intimate friend, appeared in *The Salem Gazette*, throwing interesting additional sidelights on McIntire's character as follows:

"OBITUARY NOTICE.

"Of the late and lamented Mr. M'Intire necessarily omitted in our last.

"Mr. M'Intire was originally bred to the occupation of a housewright, but his vigorous mind soon passed the ordinary limits of his profession, and aspired to the highest departments of the interesting and admirable science of architecture, in which he had advanced with a steady and sure step far beyond most of his countrymen. To a delicate native taste in this art, he had united a high degree of that polish which can only be acquired by an assiduous study of the great classical masters; with whose works, notwithstanding their rarity in this country, Mr. M. had a very intimate acquaintance. His native town (as well as other places) is enriched with many memorials in this art, whose excellences now, alas! only serve to sharpen the regret of the beholder for the loss of their author. He had also made a profession of the kindred art of sculpture, in which he had arrived at a very distinguished rank.

"The uncommon native genius of Mr. M. displayed itself in many subjects not connected with his professional pursuits; and in the various objects to which his unerring taste directed him, he never failed of reaching a degree of excellence that would have been honorable to a professed artist. He sometimes employed himself in drawing; he had an admirable musical taste, and was a good performer of instrumental as well as vocal music. Thoroughly ac-

quainted with the principles of various musical instruments, in the construction of them, particularly
the organ, the most harmonious of all, he was
directed by an ear of exquisite nicety, and an exact-
ness of mechanism that ensured success. Even on
subjects of literature his casual observations evinced
a degree of knowledge that surprised all who were
acquainted with the variety of his professional and
other pursuits. — To these attainments (and these,
notwithstanding he had been obliged to struggle
against the want of an early education, were not all
he possessed) he united an unaffected native polite-
ness, and a mildness of deportment, which delighted
all who enjoyed his acquaintance. With these rare
endowments of the mind, he possessed the best
feelings of the heart; and his exertions in the cause
of humanity (in rescuing a child from drowning)
probably laid the foundation of that disease which
had afflicted him for many years, and terminated his
life. Conspicuous among all these excellences shone
his unassuming modesty, his sterling integrity and
his ardent piety."

McIntire was laid to rest in the historic Charter
Street Burial Ground, the oldest in Salem, where lie
most of those who figured prominently in her early
history. His gravestone of dark gray slate, like

others of the time, bears a quaint inscription of comprehensive brevity, corroborating the opinions of him already expressed :

In Memory of
Mr. Samuel McIntire,
who died Feb. 6, 1811 ;
Æt. 54.

He was distinguished for Genius in Architecture,
Sculpture, and Musick : Modest and sweet Manners
rendered him pleasing : Industry and Integrity
respectable : He professed the Religion of Jesus
in his entrance on manly life; and proved its
excellence by virtuous Principles and unblemished conduct

Like his father, McIntire died intestate, his wife inheriting the property, and his son, Samuel F., continuing the business of carving and woodworking, as indicated by the following interesting advertisement which appeared in *The Salem Gazette* of April 30, 1811 :

For Sale

Sundry Articles belonging to the estate of Samuel M'Intire, deceased, — VIZ.

1 elegant Barrel Organ, 6 feet high, 10 barrels ;
1 wind chest for an organ ;
Encyclopedia complete ;
Paladia Architecture, best kind ;
1 Ware's do ; 1 Paine's do.
2 vols. French Architecture

1 large Book Antique Statues, excellent;
Lock Hospital Collection of Music;
Handel's Messiah in score;
Magdalen Hymns; Massachusetts Compiler;
1 excellent toned SPINNET,
1 excellent VIOLIN and case
1 eight day CLOCK, Mahogany case;
12 prints of the Seasons;
1 book drawings of Ships;
1 large head of Washington;
Number of Busts of the Poets;
2 Figures of Hercules, 2 feet high;
1 Head of Franklin, and Pillar for a Sign;
Composition ornaments;
Number of Moulding Planes and
sundry other Articles.   Apply to
   Elizabeth M'Intire Adm'x
  or to Samuel F. M'Intire Att'y
N. B. The subscriber carries on CARVING as usual
at the Shop of the deceased, in Summer Street where
he will be glad to receive orders in that line.   He re-
turns thanks for past favors.
April 30, 1811   Samuel F. M'Intire.

Incidentally this corroborates Bentley's obituary
and is particularly interesting as a partial list of
McIntire's library.   In addition to the works mentioned, the inventory of McIntire's property prepared by his executors includes Langley's "Architecture", "Directory of Arts and Sciences", "New
Version of New Testament", Goldsmith's "Animated
Nature", Josephus' "History", and Sandys' "Trav-

els." This inventory contains many other items of interest and may be read in full at the Essex County Probate Courthouse, book 380, page 367. It discloses the surprising fact that despite the amount and character of McIntire's prolific work, he enjoyed only moderate circumstances at the time of his death. Architecture did not command munificent fees in those days, and like many persons of artistic temperament he possessed creative ability but little capacity for accumulating money. McIntire was also generous to a fault and ever ready to help the unfortunate whom chance threw in his way. None of his relatives attained so great earning power, and there is reason to believe that he may have contributed largely in certain instances toward the betterment of their home conditions. His house and shop were appraised at three thousand dollars, probably an undervaluation, his personal property at eleven hundred and ninety dollars in addition to nine hundred and sixty-three dollars in notes. His shop was found to contain the largest equipment of carver's, joiner's, and draughtsman's tools of his time, including three hundred chisels and gouges, forty-six molding planes, and twenty large planes. A few of these tools are preserved at the Essex Institute and an examination of them redoubles one's admiration for the nicety of the work done with them.

Thus McIntire was born, lived his busy life, and died in Salem, yet he was not provincial. He never saw the best examples of Georgian architecture in England, but despite this seeming restriction and the fact that his activities were all in and about his native town, his work became favorably and forever known throughout America and even across the water, for in those days Salem was known around the globe. It has been said that he was the artistic descendant of Inigo Jones, Sir Christopher Wren, Grinling Gibbons, and the brothers Adam. So he was, and much besides. His designs are more chaste and classic than those of Wren and Gibbons, more original and imaginative than those of the brothers Adam. That his is incomparably more interesting than similar contemporaneous work elsewhere in America is due at once to his skill with tools, his mental refinement, and his native ingenuity. A man of inherent good taste and a keen sense of proportion, qualities that architects of academic training have often lacked, he had the great advantage of being able to design with the fullness of working knowledge and experience. In its painstaking thoroughness his admirable craftsmanship displays a personal pride in his work, an instinct always to do his best conscientiously for its own sake that was more nearly akin to the religious fervor which built the great cathedrals of the Middle Ages than anything known to us at present in America. Indeed, he seemed to work more directly under the strong impulse of the Renaissance, when designers reverted to the Roman classics of the fifth century, than did his more traveled and more highly educated contemporaries. The very fact that he never saw the great masterpieces of architecture appears to have sharpened and given freedom to his imagination.

Following the lead of English designers of his time less than other American workers, he oftener went back to original sources and adapted direct from Greek temples and Roman palaces, with modifications and innovations of his own. Boldly conceived, strengthened and colored by the simplicity and vigor of local conditions, these novel and clever adaptations provide the distinguishing trait of what is in many respects the most notable collection of Colonial architecture — the architecture of Salem from 1782 to 1811. Indeed, no other square mile in England or America embraces so large, so varied, or so pleasing an aggregation of the woodworker's art as was brought into being in thirty years by Samuel McIntire. This carver, designer, and architect, this building genius of Salem, died in the prime of manhood; had he been granted a normal lifetime his record of achievement would doubtless have been a far more noble one. Nevertheless every living descendant of this versatile and prolific man may take just pride in the important rôle his ancestor played in the development of our national heritage in architecture, for architects of the present day acknowledge that his woodwork presents a more domestic and delightful interpretation of Renaissance motives and therefore a more useful inspiration in modern work than any similar collection. In its freedom, refinement, lightness, and graceful dignity it is more acceptable; as an expression of the true atmosphere of the home and the gracious hospitality of the days of the early presidents, without any of its priggishness, it is more indicative.

CHAPTER III

DOORWAYS AND PORCHES

JUST as one senses something of a man by the grasp of his hand, so does one pass first judgment upon a house by its doorway, for it is the dominant exterior feature, the keynote of the façade. One never seems to disassociate a house from its entrance, so that the front doorway becomes a primary consideration in every carefully conceived design for a home; it must accord with and be worthy of the house, yet not overpower it. Narrow the proposition down to our so-called Colonial style, and we become more than ever convinced that doorways, like men, have character and individuality and so when happily devised and carefully executed will lend distinction and charm to the building as a whole. Each is important, too, as the entrance to a home; there a welcome is given and first impressions are received; it seems to symbolize the house as a whole.

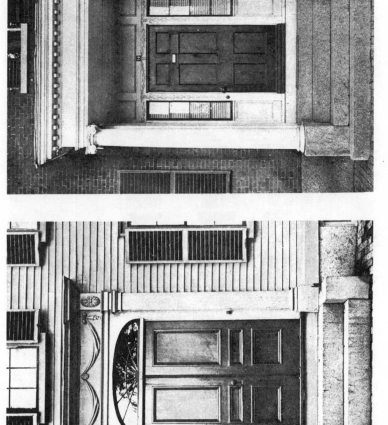

PLATE XIV.—Doorway of the Eden-Brown House; Doorway of the Kimball House.

PLATE XV.—Peabody-Silsbee House, erected in 1797.

Doorways and Porches

One has but to read history in order to realize that houses, even their doorways, reflect the character of those for whom they were built. The welcoming doorways of Salem are clothed with an indefinable something — call it atmosphere, what you will — not to be found elsewhere. Salem doorways are as broad as her merchant princes were hospitable and cultured; they seem to express a sincere spirit of democracy born of the refining influences of extensive foreign travel. Of course Salem has other doorways, such as the enclosed porch and the door without accompanying glasswork, but the wide, solid wood door with leaded side lights and elliptical fanlight, comprising one of the most attractive of the distinctive Colonial motives, is typical, as indicated by a critical study of the work of Salem's great architect.

Numerous exceptions exist, however, and the doorway of the Eden-Brown house at Number 40 Summer Street, added by McIntire in 1804 to a house then over forty years old, illustrates the occasional use of a simple elliptical fanlight without side lights. The original house was erected in 1762 for Thomas Eden, the first signer of the Salem Marine Society, established in 1766, who was a partner of that rich Marblehead merchant, Robert (commonly known as "King") Hooper because of his Tory proclivities and the fact that his beautiful country home, "The Lindens", in Danvers, was occupied by General Gage as a summer residence in 1774, while he was governor of the province of Massachusetts.

The architectural treatment of the Summer Street house recalls that given by McIntire four years previous to the enclosed porch of the Benjamin Pickman house on Essex Street, to which detailed reference will be made later in this chapter. The reeded pilasters and the festooned drapery, carved out of wood, closely resemble those of the other doorway, but here the oval florets are used as frieze spots on the pilasters and the dentil course of the cornice has been enriched by fine-scale cuttings — one vertical flute on the face of each dentil and two horizontal flutes on each side. Unfortunately, inappropriate modern doors mar the original effect.

It is a thoughtful host who provides shelter from sun and storm until his guest can be admitted, and Salem's welcome often includes the sheltering porch as well as the welcoming doorway with its friendly side lights. Such entrances possess characteristics of charm and distinction not seen elsewhere, due chiefly to their splendid proportions, refinement of detail, and precision of workmanship. Architec-

PLATE XVI.—Peabody-Silsbee Porch.

PLATE XVII.—Keyed Marble Lintel, Peabody-Silsbee House; Entablature of Window Frame, "Oak Hill."

turally the porch serves a double purpose; whereas it may lend picturesqueness to a small house, on a large house it relieves in a measure the severity of a three-story façade with many ranging windows.

Beginning with the exception rather than the rule, the Kimball house, Number 14 Pickman Street, abuts upon the sidewalk, with a porch roof over the four granite steps which rise directly from the brick pavement; there is no porch platform proper. As compared with the Eden-Brown doorway, one sees here the other extreme — the employment of side lights without a fanlight. These side lights with their square panes are of the simplest possible sort, the pleasing effect depending upon the well-proportioned door, the paneling over it, and the straight-hanging garlands on the door frame, reminiscent of the Cook-Oliver doorway, which will be described in a later chapter. Obviously, too, a porch renders any considerable embellishment of the doorway unnecessary, even superfluous. Effective simplicity characterizes this porch with its hand-carved Ionic capitals and typical entablature, conspicuous in which are the modillions under the corona with sections of fascia molding between.

Another much more elaborate instance of the Ionic porch may be seen on the Peabody-Silsbee

house, Number 380 Essex Street, of interest histori-
cally as the birthplace alike of Francis Peabody, a
close personal friend of the late J. Pierpont Morgan,
and of S. Endicott Peabody, one of the trustees of
George Peabody, the London banker for whom Peabody, Massachusetts, was named. This hip-roofed,
three-story, square house, erected in 1797, of which
McIntire was the architect, is one of his best designs
executed in brick. Both the deck roof and the belvedere on a hip roof, as in this instance, are but architectural modifications of the earlier enclosed cupola
so frequently a feature of the mansions of New
England seacoast towns. In recent years the walls
have been painted gray, but the keyed marble lintels
and sills of the windows and the white-painted woodwork remain unchanged. Although strongly Ionic
in feeling, the porch is absolutely unconventional,
and throughout the entablature shows McIntire's
bent for freshening classic motives with new detail,
or with classic detail employed in new ways. And
strangely enough, despite his daring innovations,
this porch is generally regarded as one of the best
in Salem. Could there be a higher tribute to the
genius and courage of its designer? The fluted,
nicely tapering columns, with the acanthus-leaf
enrichment of the neck of the capitals below the

PLATE XVIII.—Cornice, Eaves, and Balustraded Roof, Peabody-Silsbee House; Peabody-Silsbee Barn.

PLATE XIX.—Porch of the Stearns House.

usual volutes, impart a distinctly Roman aspect to the whole, yet the heavy, cubical Tuscan plinths were retained, and a strange, though none the less pleasing, note has been sounded by the guttæ of the Doric order both on the architrave and the mutules under the corona of the cornice. A ball molding, a veritable triumph of hand carving, replaces the customary dentil course, yet gives the same effect of scale. Thus did McIntire accomplish precedented things in unprecedented ways. The entire cornice has been repeated on a larger scale under the eaves of the house. Except for rosettes directly over the columns, the frieze is plain. The wooden door with its delicately molded panels and tiny corner ornaments; the artistic leaded fanlight and side lights, and the iron fence, stair rail, and balustrade over the porch, are all distinctive in the extreme and not surpassed by any similar work in Salem. As a whole, the effect seems actually to visualize the popular mental picture of a typical Colonial doorway.

A word may well be said in passing in regard to the stable in the rear, which, while rightly unassuming, lives in complete accord with the house, as every outbuilding should.

Roman Doric feeling pervades the porch of the Stearns house, Number 384 Essex Street, despite the cubical Tuscan plinths on which McIntire's columns of whatever order almost invariably rested. This porch was added in 1785 to a dwelling erected in 1776, and in its pediment and entablature closely resembles the front porch of the Pierce-Johonnot-Nichols house, to which detailed reference will be made in another chapter. It differs, however, in the addition of flat pilasters at each side, which give increased breadth, weight, and dignity and so in modern adaptation render it better suited to public than domestic work, unless the house be one of large size and considerable pretension.

Because of the large number of rooms and their spaciousness, the square, three-story brick mansions of the early nineteenth century lend themselves admirably to adaptation for use as semi-public institutions. Thus two splendid old dwellings, of which McIntire was the architect, now serve as the Home for Aged Women and the Woman's Friend Society respectively.

The former, at Number 180 Derby Street, was originally the residence of Benjamin W. Crowninshield, congressman and Secretary of the Navy under Presidents Madison and Monroe. When President Monroe made his tour of the North in 1817, this house was prepared for his occupancy and placed at his

PLATE XX.—Porch of the Home for Aged Women.

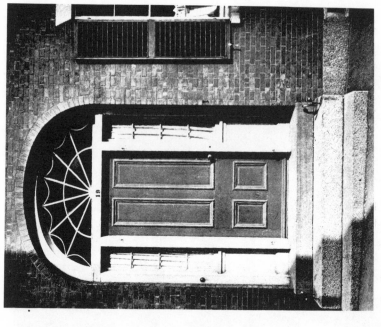

Plate XXI.—Home for Aged Women, formerly the Benjamin W. Crowninshield House, erected in 1810; Detail of Side Doorway.

disposal during the four days of his stay in Salem. At a banquet tendered to him in the southeast room on July 9, Commodores Perry and Bainbridge, Generals Miller and Dearborn, Senator Silsbee, Lieutenant-Governor William Gray, Judge Story, and other eminent men were present. Later the house became the residence of General James Miller while he was Collector of the Port from 1825 to 1849. He, it will be remembered, was the hero of Lundy's Lane, whose famous reply "I'll try, sir", was stamped on the buttons of his regiment by order of the government. In 1826, William C. Endicott, Secretary of War during Cleveland's first administration, was born here.

But it was through the generosity of a still later owner, Robert Brookhouse, a merchant who had amassed wealth in the African trade, that the house was donated outright to the Association for the Relief of Aged and Destitute Women, organized in 1860 at the suggestion of Reverend Michael Carlton, city missionary. In 1896 further donations amounting to fifty thousand dollars were expended to enlarge the structure considerably.

This hip-roofed mansion is almost devoid of ornamentation except for the marble lintels and sills of the windows and the doorways, which are Grecian

Doric of the utmost simplicity and chaste appearance, depending almost entirely for their pleasing effect upon nicety of proportion rather than enrichment of detail, and so again demonstrating McIntire's versatility. Solid wood doors, such as this, with carefully spaced and attractively molded stiles and rails, or panels as the case may be, predominate in Salem, providing an effective background for handsome brass hardware. To the very breadth of the door, and especially to the use of glass about it, as in this instance, is due the pervading spirit of welcome. Side lights encourage intimacy like hands extended in greeting; they increase the apparent breadth of the doorway and foretell a cheerful interior. Without them, a solid wood door seems to raise a barrier of reserve and superiority; the doorway seems narrower, and the fanlight indicates the desire for more illumination without the willingness to descend to the equality of the passer-by to obtain it. Who shall say, then, that in his choice of a doorway the prospective home builder does not reflect his own personality and mental attitude toward his fellow men? Certainly his course is clear, whether he would encourage friendship with his neighbors or maintain toward them an attitude of distant exclusiveness.

PLATE XXII.—Clifford Crowninshield House, erected in 1805; Pickman-Derby-Brookhouse Estate, erected in 1764.

Plate XXIII.—Clifford Crowninshield Porch; Gardner-White-Pingree Porch.

Doorways and Porches

Those who know the annals of Salem commerce will recall that the first Salem vessel to circumnavigate the globe was the *Minerva*, owned by Clifford Crowninshield and Nathaniel West. By such daring ventures did the former accumulate the wealth which made possible the erection of his home at Number 74 Washington Square in 1805. Aside from its ample size and excellent interior finish, it is really a hiproofed dwelling of the utmost simplicity, and the porch over the front doorway affords the only architectural embellishment, other than the necessary windows, to break the great expanse of the façade. As a type, this entrance with its heavy Tuscan columns is the forerunner of the tasteful semi-oval porch which was evolved by McIntire when he realized the possibilities of a slender interpretation of the Corinthian column and entablature. The simple grace of the fence, with its small, square posts, light, molded rail and base, and unique jig-sawed member between each five square pickets, provides an effective foil for the severity of the house itself, the form it takes each side of the porch being especially appropriate in this instance.

Two excellent examples of the semi-oval Corinthian porch just referred to may be compared as found on the Tucker-Rice house, Number 129 Essex Street, erected in 1800, and in the Gardner-White-Pingree house, Number 128 Essex Street, erected in 1810, both designed by McIntire. The latter was, perhaps, McIntire's last work. It is conceded to be his best brick house and contains remarkably fine interior finish. Exteriorly, by the ingenious expedient of applying broad, horizontal bands of white marble at each floor level, McIntire demonstrated how simple a matter it is to relieve the severity of so high a façade. These bands, together with the marble sills and keyed lintels of the many ranging windows, contribute much toward a seemingly broader frontage and so, like the foreshortened third-story windows, tend to reduce the apparent total height. A comparison of this with the Tucker-Rice house also discloses more fully the effectiveness of a balustraded roof quite apart from its ornamental value. Instead of increasing the seeming height, it has the very contrary effect, and by placing the roof line somewhat below the absolute top of the structure causes the whole mass to look lower.

The Tucker-Rice porch was much admired by Professor Eleazer B. Homer, of the Massachusetts Institute of Technology summer school, who told his class in 1895, while in Salem, that it was the best proportioned porch in the city. And so it remains

PLATE XXIV.—Porch of the Tucker-Rice House.

PLATE XXV.—Tucker-Rice House, erected in 1800; Detail of Porch.

to-day, although its former beauty of ensemble has been marred by the substitution of inappropriate modern doors and surrounding glasswork. Its neighbor across the street, however, still displays the charming, original leaded glass and the quaint door, three panels wide, which became such a popular feature of the doorways of 1818, but the columns of this porch are not fluted in the characteristic Corinthian manner. As one sees these porches to-day, the ideal lies in a mental composite of the two, which would be very nearly what the Tucker-Rice porch originally was. Indeed, despite the elaboration of the type by the builders of 1818, nothing was accomplished to surpass this supreme achievement in grace, delicacy, and refinement; the detail is almost beyond criticism and the proportions such as to make instant appeal to any seeing eye.

Other differences occur in the entablatures, the moldings of the Tucker-Rice porch being worked to a finer scale, though in this it adheres less closely to precedent. It will be seen that in each instance the cornice with its jig-sawed modillions has been repeated on a larger scale under the eaves of the house. The iron fences and stair rails interest the antiquary as contrasting the wrought iron of the older house with the cast iron of the newer. The former repeats well-known Florentine motives always welcome, whereas the latter bespeaks admiration for the apparent stability, yet light and decorative effect, of the square, openwork gateposts. Both the Tucker-Rice doorway and porch are now preserved on the grounds of the Essex Institute, the lower floor recently having been remodeled.

The semi-oval porch was also a feature of two other notable houses of McIntire design no longer in existence. One of these, shown by an old print reproduced on another page, stood on the site now occupied by the museum building of the Essex Institute, which, before the extensive alterations of 1906, had been Plummer Hall, the quarters of the Salem Athenæum. Few spots in this historic city recall as many interesting associations with the events and personages of bygone days. Here was located the house of Emanuel Downing who married a sister of Governor John Winthrop. Downing Street, London, now a synonym for the official residence of the Prime Minister, was named for their son, George Downing, the diplomatist, while Downing College, Cambridge, derived its name from his grandson. George Downing's daughter married Captain Joseph Gardner, the "Fighting Joe" of the Narraganset wars. From this very house he set forth for the "Great Swamp

PLATE XXVI.—Gardner-White-Pingree House, erected in 1810.

PLATE XXVII.—Detail of Gardner-White-Pingree Porch.

Fight" in 1675, during which he was killed. His widow married Governor Simon Bradstreet who lived here in his old age and died here. In later years this estate was for generations the homestead of the famous Bowditch family until the last dwelling on the site was built from plans by McIntire in 1790 for Honorable Nathan Read, a congressman. On May 4, 1796, William Hickling Prescott, the historian, whose "Conquest of Mexico" is known to most readers of the English language, was born in this house, which in 1799 became the residence of Captain Joseph Peabody, a wealthy merchant prominent in the Calcutta trade, whose ship *George* made twenty-one voyages to that port, $651,743.32 in duties being paid into the Salem Custom-house on her cargoes. It was upon the death of Captain Peabody's widow that the estate was purchased by the Salem Athenæum. The old mansion was razed in 1856, and Plummer Hall was erected in 1857.

The other McIntire house, formerly at Number 151 Lafayette Street, was built for Josiah Dow in 1787, and was afterwards known as the Osgood estate. In later years it was occupied by John F. Hurley, a recent mayor of Salem, until razed in 1909 to make way for the French Catholic Parish House. The original house of brick, three stories high and hip-

roofed, was one of those picturesque, end-to-the-
street arrangements, with the front door opening
upon the yard at one side, and the ell, shed, and
barn with their arched doorways and balustraded
roof rambling away to the rear. The white marble
sills and keyed lintels of the twelve-paned Georgian
windows lent character, dignity, and scale to the exterior, and its crowning feature, the entrance —
porch and doorway — was evidently done by Mc-
Intire in the fullness of his artistic powers. The
door, topped and flanked with delightful leaded
glasswork, possesses all the chaste and delightful
charm of the Benjamin W. Crownishield door, while
the semi-oval Tuscan porch has not been excelled in
effective simplicity. The high picket fence with its
modest ornamental gates, particularly that over
which an arch of Florentine bent iron formerly sus-
pended a lantern, was ever much admired. The
splendid posts, surmounted with hand-tooled spheres
and otherwise molded and enriched with fluted pilasters and carved Ionic capitals, have frequently been
copied by architects for modern work.

At the much-used side door, the enclosed porch
became a distinctive feature of the early New England mansion; it was the forerunner of the modern
vestibule, which does so much toward ensuring

PLATE XXVIII.—Nathan Reed House, erected 1790; Josiah Dow House, erected 1787.

PLATE XXIX.—Hosmer-Waters Enclosed Porch and Front Doorway.

warm interiors in winter. The most frequent conception of it took the form of a pediment supported by pilasters with a solid wood door having rails and molded panels spaced according to the characteristic manner of the time, and oval windows in the sides to admit light. A charming example is to be seen on the Hosmer-Waters house, Number 80 Washington Square, designed for Captain Joseph Hosmer by McIntire in 1795, and rendered more picturesque with the passing years by a giant wistaria which regularly clothes it with a wealth of bloom in springtime. In this instance fluted pilasters accompany a simple Tuscan pediment, and the combination has stood the test of years, being one of the most admired doorways in Salem. The harmonious relation yet slight difference between this and the front door of the same house offer interesting material for comparison. A similar enclosed porch on the Pierce-Johonnot-Nichols house illustrates the employment of a Doric pediment with the repeated triglyph in the frieze and guttæ in the architrave.

The flat-roofed, enclosed porch of the David P. Waters house, Number 14 Cambridge Street, is unusual in its breadth, due to the employment of the ever-charming side lights beside the door rather than oval sashes in the side walls common to most of the other enclosed porches of Salem. McIntire imparted further individuality by adopting the broad two-part door three panels wide. Supported by fine-scale fluted pilasters, the entablature is generally Corinthian in character and includes a hand-tooled dentil course with modillions supporting the corona.

About 1800 McIntire added an enclosed porch of more picturesque type to the gambrel-roofed house of Benjamin Pickman, the elder, who, in 1756, was Judge of the Superior Court and Colonel of the Salem regiment at the same time. Erected in 1743, the house still stands in the rear of Number 165 Essex Street, partly concealed by stores, but the interior has been despoiled of its beautiful woodwork which illustrated well the tendencies of the pre-Revolutionary period and was particularly interesting because of the carved and gilded codfish on each stair end, indicating the source of the owner's wealth. The archway through which one passes from the picture gallery into the museum of the Essex Institute was taken from this house. Among the distinguished guests entertained here were Governor Pownall, October 22, 1757, Count Castiglioni, June 23, 1784, and Alexander Hamilton, June 20, 1800.

This McIntire porch takes somewhat the form of the modern cottage bay window with supporting reeded pilasters, which also provide the neck of the capitals, oval windows in the sides to admit light, and a surmounting cornice and frieze to which the designer apparently devoted special attention. The festooned drapery and oval florets of the frieze are carved out of wood, and the cavetto molding of the cornice, suggesting a series of tiny arches, contributes a novel bit of handwork not found in other McIntire designs. The present door, of course, is obviously modern and inappropriate.

It was for Benjamin Pickman, Jr., a wealthy merchant, that the brick mansion at Number 70 Washington Street, later known as the Pickman-Derby-Brookhouse estate, was built in 1764, replacing the large wooden house of Reverend Nicholas Noyes, who was extremely violent in the witch trials of 1692. Later it became the residence of Elias Haskett Derby, who occupied it during the best years of his life until, in 1799 and shortly before his death, he moved into his eighty thousand dollar mansion designed by McIntire. The accompanying photograph shows the house as it appeared before its removal to make way for the present Masonic Temple. The wood trim, including the Ionic pilasters, balustrade of the roof, cupola and hand-carved eagle in wood, also the barn, were added by McIntire during Derby's occupancy. The festooned drapery on the barn was transferred to the barn of Mr. John Robinson, Number 18 Summer Street, and the cupola to the grounds of the Essex Institute where it may now be seen. On the arched ceiling of the cupola a fresco by Corné depicted the several vessels of the Derby fleet, and in the blind of one of the windows a hole was left through which a telescope could be pointed to watch for ships. John Rogers the sculptor was born in this house, October 30, 1829.

It is with genuine admiration that we look to-day upon these famous old doorways of Salem, not only because they have furnished the inspiration for and are the equal of the best recent work, but because they are entirely of wood, hand-tooled out of white pine, and we realize full well how crude were the tools of those days and how essential the utmost of patient, painstaking, and skilful workmanship. With their graceful dignity and simple air of distinction these old doorways are well worth the study of every prospective home builder; they cannot fail to appeal strongly to any thinking person of good taste and refinement having a ready appreciation of our national traditions.

PLATE XXX.—David P. Waters Enclosed Porch; Benjamin Pickman Enclosed Porch.

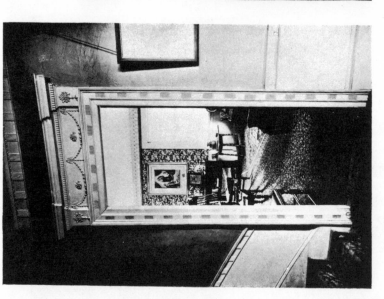

PLATE XXXI.—Parlor Doorway of Clifford Crowninshield Hall; Door in Derby-Crowninshield-Rogers House.

CHAPTER IV

INTERIOR WOODWORK

WHITE–PAINTED wood finish provides the only thoroughly satisfactory setting for mahogany furniture, now, as in McIntire's day, the popular ideal in American homes. Nothing to excel the slender Sheraton and Adam elegance or the more substantial beauty of Chippendale and Heppelwhite designs has been devised by the furniture makers of more recent times. Executed in dark woods, whether mahogany, rosewood, or walnut, these four justly famous types possess rare grace of line, nicety of detail, and richness of effect which are enhanced by a background of white standing finish. The interior woodwork provides the setting in which the furniture gems of a room are placed. Just as the row of white pearls sets off to best advantage the richness of the ruby or emerald, so white-painted woodwork serves as a foil to emphasize the mellow warmth and graceful dignity of dark eighteenth-century furniture, forceful in its contrast and cheerful in its brightening effect. The same pieces would lose half their charm in a room having dark wood trim. Indeed, few woods available for interior finish harmonize with mahogany furniture when waxed or varnished in their natural colors. And while there is a somber richness about mahogany finish and furniture combined, both together seem undesirable, except for an occasional room in a large and pretentious house.

We realize now as never before that our great-grandfathers displayed excellent taste in placing their rare pieces of furniture, brought from across the seas, in white-trimmed rooms. This treatment has stood the test of time, and with the recurring popularity of architecture and other things Colonial, is again finding the favor it really deserves. It is not surprising, therefore, that to examine the photographs of recent houses designed by almost any ten well-known American architects is to be impressed by the predominance of the Colonial spirit which pervades the principal rooms. The lure of white-painted interior woodwork is upon us; prospective home builders of education and artistic tastes are demanding it, and intelligent architects are happy indeed to comply, even in the case of houses

PLATE XXXII.—Stucco Cornice in Derby-Crowninshield-Rogers House; Wainscot and Surbase.

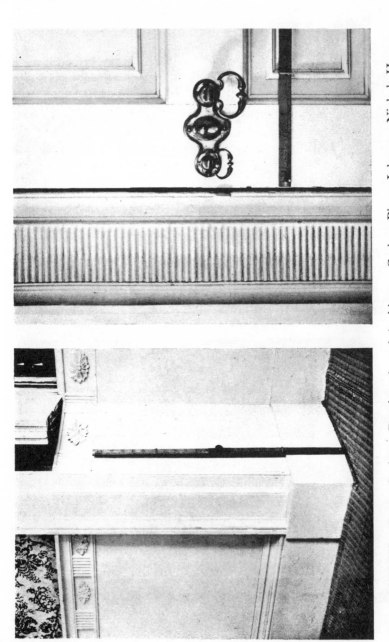

PLATE XXXIII.—Dado, Surbase, Baseboard, and Architrave Casing, Pierce-Johonnot-Nichols House; Door Paneling, Casing, and Drop Handle.

which in exterior appearance and constructive materials disregard period. This is because it harks back to early traditions which we at once respect and admire.

There is a certain financial psychology about it, too. White pine, once the cheapest of native woods, has been used with such prodigality and for so many purposes that in finish grades, although obtainable in ample quantity from the Northwest, it now costs as much as some good hardwoods. Unfortunately human nature too often permits us to measure the worth of an article by the price which supply and demand have placed upon it. Now that white pine has become expensive because of its scarcity in the East, we have begun to prize it highly. And then, too, we have had an opportunity to observe its sterling qualities in the remarkably well preserved old mansions of our early seaport towns.

McIntire's admirable work in Salem affords eloquent testimony to the fact that the possibilities of painted softwood for interior finish are fully as great as those of more expensive hardwoods. Effects must be achieved in a different way, however. The broad, flat surfaces and simple moldings of hardwood finish depend for their interest chiefly upon the natural grain of the wood. Painting similar designs executed in softwood would conceal the grain and leave them uninteresting and without character. Painted wood finish needs beauty of form as a substitute for the beauty of wood grain. Lest the background become monotonous and unworthy of its furniture accompaniments, therefore, the motives and details of exterior ornamentation, such as moldings, carefully spaced panels, and appropriate carving, or its equivalent in applied ornament, are brought to bear upon the interior woodwork in such a manner as to delight the eye, yet not to detract unduly from the contents of the room. To this end a nice balance between plain surface and decoration is as important as the decoration itself. Fireplaces and stairways, the principal architectural features of interiors, properly may be elaborated considerably beyond the somewhat negative character of background accessories. Tasteful ornamentation applied to such important forms of utility and necessity seems sincere and amply justified. Indeed, they are regarded almost as furnishings rather than parts of the house.

For convenience in studying them, Colonial interiors may well be divided into three classes: first, those having a molded baseboard and a simple picture molding or cornice; second, those of which a

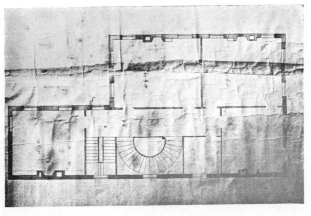

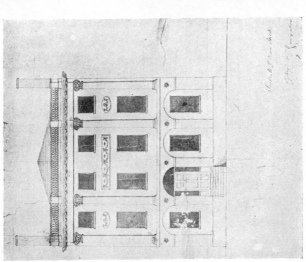

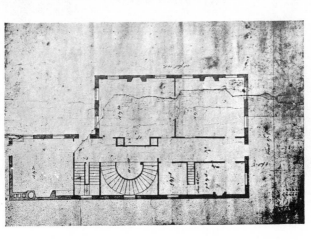

PLATE XXXIV.—Street Floor Plan, Derby-Crowninshield-Rogers House; Front Elevation; Second Floor Plan.

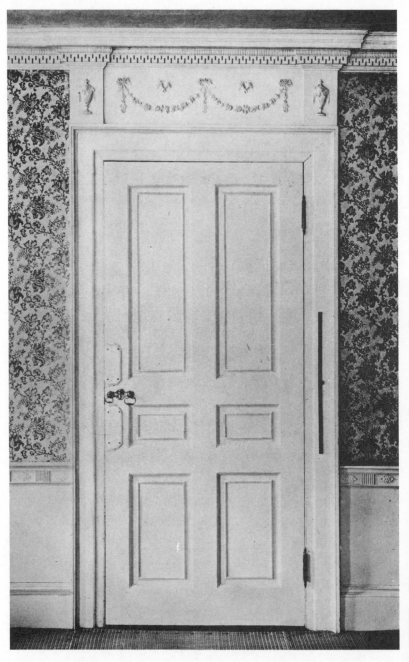

PLATE XXXV.—Doorway in East Front Chamber, Pierce-Johonnot-
Nichols House.

dado or paneled wainscot, almost invariably accompanied by a cornice, is a feature; third, those rooms architecturally treated with paneled walls.

McIntire seldom employed the first of these treatments. The hall at "Oak Hill", the summer home of Mrs. J. C. Rogers at Peabody, Massachusetts, erected in 1800, appears to be the only instance of consequence. Although appropriate in any room of a small house, architects of the present day often reserve it, because of its extreme simplicity, for chambers and unimportant rooms not often seen by outsiders. As in this instance the cornice, accompanied by a flat frieze, but without the architrave, is used with a molded baseboard.

The second, and McIntire's favorite treatment, combining dado and cornice, has proved itself generally useful, especially in hall, dining room, living room, and the principal bedrooms of large houses.

As an exemplification of the classic orders applied to interior woodwork, it is especially interesting and consistent; the dado, the wall above it, and the cornice corresponding to the pedestal, shaft, and entablature respectively. When this treatment is applied to a room, the dado becomes in very truth a continuous pedestal with a plinth and base molding and a surbase surmounting the die or plane face of the pedestal. Suggesting a miniature cornice, this surbase may be molded horizontally, as in most of the rooms at "Oak Hill", or attractively elaborated with vertical hand-carved reedings or flutings on a fascia-like band below the surbase proper. These reedings may be continuous, as in the hall of the Cook-Oliver house, or in groups of seven or so with sections of plain fascia between them, as in the Clifford Crowninshield house. Again, the surbase may be still further enriched by a circular or oval floret, carved or in composition, applied in alternation with the reeded groups, as in the Derby-Crowninshield-Rogers house, Number 202½ Essex Street, and the east front chamber of the Pierce-Johonnot-Nichols house. As seen in the east parlor of the latter delightful old mansion, McIntire sometimes used vertical fluted instead of reeded groups to ornament the surbase, while in several rooms of the old house at Number 202½ Essex Street and also in the drawing-room at "Oak Hill" the well-known and always welcome Grecian fret, that favorite motive that so often replaces the dentil course of his cornices, lends distinction to the surbase.

The histories of the two houses last mentioned are so closely interwoven that it seems well to digress momentarily in order to recount them in a single

PLATE XXXVI.—Drawing-Room Doorway, "Oak Hill."

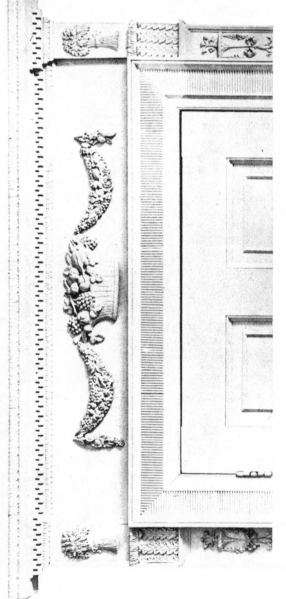

PLATE XXXVII.—Detail of Doorway of a Chamber at "Oak Hill."

brief paragraph. Both in exterior appearance and interior arrangement, as shown by McIntire's accompanying floor plans and elevation, the Derby-Crowninshield-Rogers house holds much of interest to the student and architect in that it was originally an early type of the modern town house. Shortly after its erection about 1800, it was occupied by Ezekiel Hersey Derby, a son of Elias Haskett Derby, Salem's greatest merchant. Not having the family love of adventures at sea, however, he soon moved to the family estate in South Salem, there to devote himself to the pursuits of agriculture. His town house then became the last residence in Salem of Benjamin W. Crowninshield before moving to Boston. It was last occupied as a winter residence by Richard S. Rogers, a wealthy merchant in the foreign trade, whose splendid summer home on a farm in Peabody, also designed by McIntire, is now known as "Oak Hill" and occupied as a summer residence by his son's widow, Mrs. J. C. Rogers. "Oak Hill" was built originally for Nathaniel West, a wealthy merchant and ship owner, who married Elizabeth Derby, one of the daughters of Elias Haskett Derby. When the old Salem residence became the Maynes estate, the street floor was converted into stores, and so it stands to-day a mere echo of its pristine elegance yet still admired by those who know and appreciate good architecture.

While these old dados are of the low type with a plain wood face, in modern work a similar effect is sometimes obtained in dining rooms by the simple expedient of a baseboard and surbase at the same height as the top of the chair backs with a papered wall between. Still another device to carry the wood-work high on dining room walls of the present day is to adopt the paneled wainscot so often executed in hardwood and equally if not more effective when of softwood painted white. Preferably five or six feet high, this may be surmounted by a plate rail or only a heavy molding as preferred.

When accompanying a dado, the cornice may properly be of more distinctive character, with a prominent denticulated molding replacing the corona, as in the hall at "Oak Hill" and in several rooms at Number 202½ Essex Street, or considerably elaborated by hand carving after the Adam manner, as in the morning room at "Oak Hill." There the Grecian fret reappears supplemented by a broad frieze beneath, consisting of a continuous band of vertical reedings. In the drawing-room of the same house reeded groups alternate with circular medallions set in square plain sections of the frieze to form a richer effect.

PLATE XXXVIII.—Doorway of the Morning Room, "Oak Hill."

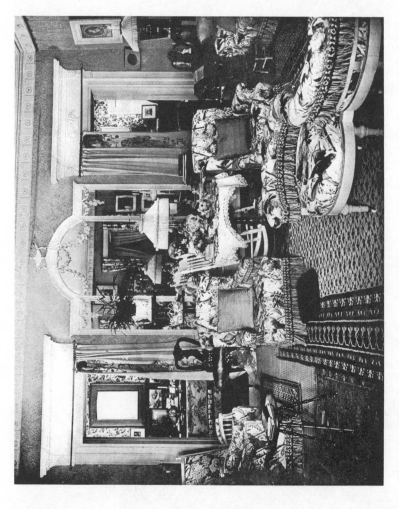

PLATE XXXIX.—Architectural Treatment of the Drawing-Room, "Oak Hill."

A novel and interesting variation of the cornice may be seen in the hall of the Clifford Crowninshield house.   Below the usual cyma recta a reeding, hand-tooled spirally and resembling the twist drills of to-day, though doubtless a modification of the popular rope moldings of the time, replaces the usual flat fillet. The corona with a plain torus below it has been given the width of a narrow frieze, and its flat surface relieved at intervals with groups of seven vertical reedings corresponding to those of the sur-base. Another cornice of still different character in the Derby-Crowninshield-Rogers house consists entirely of plaster-work according to designs by McIntire, including well-known classic detail of which the egg and tongue molding, scroll and in-terlacing circular fillet frets are prominent.

Most pretentious of all, the third treatment of completely paneled walls with embrasured windows best creates the atmosphere of formal rooms, such as hall, reception room, or dining room. Purely as a matter of convenience in the library it sometimes serves attractively to fill the spaces between and above built-in bookcases, doors, and windows. Pan-eling is a true measure of an architect's skill in ap-propriate spacing; a subtle sense of proportion and careful selection of moldings are necessary. No examples exist to-day to indicate that McIntire ever completely paneled any of his interiors, as did some of the English builders who came to America prior to the Revolution. Paneling one of the four walls of a room, however, was a picturesque custom of the time often adopted by him and revived occasionally to-day. This architectural treatment was usually resorted to when a fireplace was flanked by a door at each side, one often opening into a closet and the other into an adjoining room. Notable examples are found in the Pierce-Johonnot-Nichols house. These same rooms show McIntire's application of embrasured windows with folding shutters and window seats to unpaneled walls. In a dining room a clever modern adaptation of the same idea consists of paneling carried around a small oriel window and extended on each side to corner china closets with arched, leaded glass doors. Such an application of white-painted woodwork brightens the space about a window and makes cheerful a portion of the room that too often seems dark and gloomy.

In any scheme of interior woodwork, windows and doors naturally attract particular notice. McIntire's windows were usually of the twelve-paned Georgian type which still continues to find favor in

PLATE XL.—Inside of Front Doorway, "Oak Hill."

PLATE XLI.—Two Views of the Second Floor Hall, "Oak Hill,"
showing Zuber's "Classic" Wall Paper.

most Colonial adaptations. With a few exceptions, such as the east parlor of the Pierce-Johonnot-Nichols house, the casings indoors as well as outside were molded after the manner of an architrave, with the window sill at the level of the surbase and the casing across the lintel joining the cornice or being somewhat below, according to the height of the room. The casings of less important doorways were the same, while those in more conspicuous positions, like those at the foot of the stairs at "Oak Hill", were elaborated by the addition of a beautiful cornice and frieze which, with the architrave motive of the lintel, form a complete entablature. The cornice of this doorhead includes one beautifully hand-carved molding with tiny spheres between the dentils, and is supported by pilasters each side of the frieze. A dainty applied grape cluster decorates each pilaster, and a superbly modeled fruit basket within an oval, beaded border, also applied, occupies the center of the broad frieze.

Similar doorways are to be seen in the Clifford Crowninshield and Derby-Crowninshield-Rogers houses, in both of which the decorations of the door-head frieze consist of applied work in the form of dainty festooned and straight-hanging garlands with florets between and Adam urns or ornamental flower-

pots with blooming plants on the pilasters supporting the cornice in which a hand-tooled dentil
course invariably is prominent. As in the Pierce-
Johonnot-Nichols house, several of the doorways of
the Clifford Crowinshield house have casings with
groups of flutings at frequent intervals, and in
the east front chamber of the Pierce-Johonnot-
Nichols house a doorway demonstrates how pleasingly the cornice of the room and that of the doorhead may be one and the same in low-studded
rooms.

Although with few exceptions McIntire's moldings
were planed and carved by hand, most of the more
elaborate decorations of doorheads and chimney
pieces, such as baskets, urns, garlands, and cornu-
copias were molded in French putty, applied to the
surface of the wood with glue, and painted. After
more than a century these ornaments, as found at
"Oak Hill", still remain in perfect condition, indicating that leading decorators of the present time
make no mistake in continuing to use this form of
ornamentation.

Other more elaborate doorways at "Oak Hill",
three of which are illustrated herewith, have a considerable amount of applied ornament. Outside
the casings, upon which hand-tooled reedings are

PLATE XLII.—Hall and Stairway at "Oak Hill."

PLATE XLIII.—Elliptical Arches in the Hall, Derby-Crowninshield-Rogers House.

cut, either molded or fluted pilasters rise from projecting bases, corresponding to the baseboard, to the doorhead. The applied capitals represent variously modified forms of the Corinthian order, in which the acanthus leaf motive is prominent, while in the sunken panels of the pilasters the straight-hanging garland effect is a feature interspersed with other delicate, fine-scale ornament. Fruit-filled urns or sheaves of wheat decorate the pilasters supporting the cornices, and fruit baskets, urns, and festoons fill the friezes. Two of the moldings of each cornice are examples of refined applied work in which the acanthus and Lesbian leaves predominate, and a hand-tooled Grecian fret supplies the dentil course between them.

Quaint in appearance, the old six-panel doors are attractively arranged with four panels of equal size and two small ones at the top, according to McIntire's favorite manner. Both stiles and the muntin are of equal width, but the lock and bottom rails are broader than the top and frieze rails. In most instances moldings are confined to the edges of the panels, but in the drawing-room an additional molding has been applied to the panel itself, about an inch from the edge, recalling the doors of the Derby-Crowninshield-Rogers and the later portion of the

Pierce-Johonnot-Nichols houses. The latter instance also illustrates McIntire's variation in panel arrangement, the small panels being happily placed between the larger ones which, in consequence, are of unequal size, the larger pair being at the top. Stiles, muntin, and rails are here alike except for the broader bottom rail. In the older portion of this house and also in the Cook-Oliver house the panels are nicely beveled. No finer examples of the quaint and elegant drop handle as a substitute for the more common round brass knob of that day are to be found in America than those in the Pierce-Johonnot-Nichols house, which have several times been reproduced in recent works.

Returning once more to "Oak Hill", one side of the drawing-room, architecturally treated, illustrates more convincingly than any similar instance known to the authors the splendid possibilities of white wood finish; it is the equal of the chimney piece end of the Pierce-Johonnot-Nichols east parlor and hence one of McIntire's supreme achievements. Two doorways, similar to those already described, are located at opposite sides of the wall, while a large mirror in the same spirit occupies the space between. In three parts, the broad central portion has a segmental top, and the narrower flanking portions have

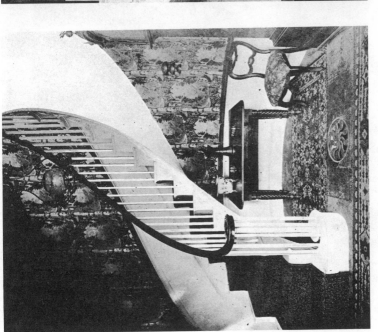

PLATE XLIV.—"Winder" in the David P. Waters House; Stairway in the Hosmer-Waters House.

PLATE XLV.—Side Stairway, Pierce-Johonnot-Nichols House; Back Stairway, Derby-Crowninshield-Rogers House.

horizontal tops. These tops take the form of a cornice and frieze, echoing those of the room itself, with applied medallions at regular intervals and hand-tooled vertical flutings substituted for the reedings above. A delicately executed urn surmounts the central mirror and from it hang graceful festoons of applied work over the glass. Molded pilasters with applied garlands in their sunken panels serve as mullions or casings. The whole effect is one of rare beauty, refined, distinctive, a tribute to McIntire's good taste and exceptional sense of proportion. Indicating clearly the influence of the brothers Adam upon his work, it is still no mere copy of their designs, but is possessed of marked individuality.

A wealth of suggestion lies in the front doorway with its well-proportioned fanlight and side lights. Here one sees the interior charm of the typical Colonial front doorway arrangement. One notices with interest that the charming pattern in these particular sashes is obtained by the use of iron bent against the glass rather than by means of sash bar divisions. Unfortunately the modern door is not in accord with others in the house, but the original finish, including reeded pilasters with modified Corinthian capitals, a lintel with hand-tooled flutings, and an elliptical arch with frieze motive of reeded sections between applied florets, is splendid.

As in most houses of this period, the elliptical arch of the fanlight is echoed elsewhere, sometimes supported by pilasters and framing the stairway vista or that at the far end of a long hall, as in this instance; also frequently spanning the upper hall at the head of the stairs where it rests upon beautifully carved consoles. It may also be seen at intersections of hall corridors in the Derby-Crowninshield-Rogers house. This brings us to a consideration of the Colonial hall, ever of great interest as an avenue of approach from the doorway to the fireside, and its principal embellishment, the stairway.

Stairways provide opportunities for architectural treatment quite as spontaneous and admirable as do chimney pieces, and McIntire's work includes virtually all of the really satisfactory types. In the old residences of Salem, wide halls sometimes lead completely through the center of the house with an outside door at both ends and doors at each side giving access to the principal rooms, as in the Cook-Oliver house. Oftener, as at "Oak Hill" and in the Pierce-Johonnot-Nichols house, halls extend only part way through the house, the rear door opening

PLATE XLVI.—"Winder" in the Derby-Crowninshield-Rogers House.

PLATE XLVII.—Stairway at Second Floor Level, Derby-Crowninshield-Rogers House; Detail of Newel and Stair Ends.

into a room rather than into the yard or garden. Where the balustrade is considerably elaborated, a simple molded baseboard runs about the walls and up the stairway, but oftener there is a dado like that in the David P. Waters hall. The paneled wainscot of the pre-Revolutionary builders appears not to have appealed to McIntire, although some paneling occurs in the Derby-Crowninshield-Rogers house.

In long halls the stairway takes the form of a single straight run, as at "Oak Hill", or of a straight run to a landing only three or four steps below the second-floor level where the direction of the flight reverses. On this landing, as in the Cook-Oliver and Pierce-Johonnot-Nichols houses, a beautiful Palladian window admits light and provides an effective feature of the architectural scheme. At opposite sides of the window in bygone days often stood a floor clock and a tip-table on which were placed the candles to light guests to bed. In short halls a broken flight with two landings at opposite sides of the hall where right angle turns occur was less popular about 1800 than now. Although it had been the prevailing type in the mansions of 1750, and was used with heavy turned balusters in the Hosmer-Waters house, erected in 1795, McIntire ordinarily reserved it for the side or rear stairway, as in the Pierce-Johonnot-Nichols or Derby-Crowinshield-Rogers houses. He seemed to prefer the more graceful and striking semi-circular stairway or "winder" as a solution of the short hall problem. A particularly pleasing example occurs in the David P. Waters house, and it may be seen on a much more ambitious scale in the old mansion at Number 202½ Essex Street, already referred to many times.

These stairways of whatever type depend in large measure for their beauty and distinction upon the ornamentation of balustrade, dado, and stair ends. Although occasionally painted white, a dark-stained pine or mahogany molded handrail is the rule. Usually it curves outward to the newel at the bottom and occasionally winds about in spiral fashion on a broad, bottom stair, suggesting the volute of the Ionic order, the stair tread taking the shape of the rail above, as in the David P. Waters house. Upward, the rail sometimes swings along from flight to flight, unbroken by newels, as in the Pierce-Johonnot-Nichols house, or again, at each landing and floor, sweeps upward in a graceful curve to a newel, as illustrated by the back stairway of the Derby-Crowninshield-Rogers house. When accompanied by a dado as in the Hosmer-Waters hall, its surbase

PLATE XLVIII.—Detail of Newel and Twisted Balusters, "Oak Hill."

PLATE XLIX.—A Doorway in the Hall, "Oak Hill."

duplicated this graceful sweep of the ramped rail. McIntire's balustrades afford slender turned newels and balusters of several attractive patterns, while the stairway of the David P. Waters house indicates the charm of simple inch-square balusters when applied to a stairway the very form of which provides its own ornament. Almost invariably some form of scroll brackets under the overhang of the tread lent a note of individuality, and sometimes this was supplemented by the application of some form of restrained yet highly effective decoration along the second-floor level, such as the fret in the Pierce-Johonnot-Nichols house, and the applied festooned garlands and oval florets in the Derby-Crowninshield-Rogers house.

Built during the days of our maritime supremacy, many houses, of which "Oak Hill" is an example, were influenced considerably in their decorative details by the shipbuilding industry. This is seen particularly in the stairway with its paneled box-stairs and beautifully turned and carved balusters and newels which were suggested by the rope moldings much used in the ship cabins of those days. Three balusters stand on each stair, the twisted portion of each being different, although the turned portions at the top and bottom are all alike. The newel is a particularly good specimen of its type and consists of one corkscrew spiral within another, a difficult and excellent piece of hand carving indicating the native ingenuity and intuitive decorative sense of the skilled craftsmen to whom so great a measure of the charm of Salem architecture is due.

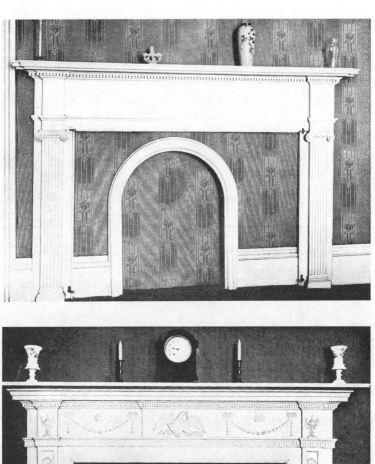

PLATE L.—Mantel in a Chamber of the Hosmer-Waters House;
Mantel in Northwest Parlor.

PLATE LI.—Parlor Mantel, Lindall-Barnard-Andrews House; Corner
Section showing hand carved Applied Ornament.

CHAPTER V

MANTELS AND CHIMNEY PIECES

A FIREPLACE ever makes a strong sentimental appeal, not only for the charm of the open fire, but because it seems to represent the ideal of homely comfort in the days when people lived close to the hearthstone; it is human and direct. A century ago the fireplace was the source of warmth and good cheer during six months of the year and the very center of home life; here the family gathered when the day's work was done; here the honored guest was entertained; here youth plighted troth, and plans for new firesides were whispered in the mellow glow from the hearth. The fireplace was a thing of the utmost necessity that could be made beautiful by the application of woodwork with carving and other embellishment. Naturally, therefore, like the architects of all times, McIntire devoted his best efforts to the judicious ornamentation of his mantels and chimney pieces; they became the crowning feature of his interiors, indeed virtually the keynote of the scheme of furnishing and decoration, and, because of McIntire's rare skill and creative genius, they are possessed of exceptional grace of line and proportion.

To contemplate these masterpieces of interior woodwork is to comprehend the importance and attributes of the fireplace. Unlike many architects of the present day McIntire realized fully that while sentiment lies in the fire on the hearth, the fire is absent during warm weather, and that as a permanent ornamental feature of the house actual beauty centers not in the fireplace proper but in its architectural setting, the mantel or entire chimney piece. Hence he invariably avoided structural materials that would have emphasized the fireplace opening by strong color-contrast with the white woodwork, such as red brick facings with conspicuous mortar joints. Instead, he employed marble, white and of various tints and markings, gray soapstone, and the like, a precedent in close harmony which may well be followed to-day.

Many of McIntire's mantels were very simple, yet never deficient in that chaste appearance and just proportion which characterized all his work. An interesting one, intended as the setting for a

PLATE LII.—Mantel in the West Chamber of the Peabody-Silsbee House.

PLATE LIII.—Mantel in the Rear Parlor of the Woman's Bureau.

Mantels and Chimney Pieces

Franklin stove, may be seen in a chamber of the Hosmer-Waters house. Like numerous others made entirely of wood, the frieze beneath the shelf is plain, and the hand tooling has been confined to the fluted pilasters with Ionic capitals and two moldings of the cornice. The dentil course displays typical McIntire traits to be seen elsewhere, and a realistic rope molding carved with painstaking care replaces the conventional ovolo.

At the outset of McIntire's independent career, and occasionally for ten years or so afterward, considerable of the enrichment of the mantel frieze was carved in wood and applied with glue, as in the case of the delightful mantel made in 1800 for the Lindall-Barnard-Andrews house, Number 393 Essex Street, erected in 1747. McIntire's personal carving here includes not only the central basket of fruit and flowers, but the festoons, sheaves of wheat, the delicate cuttings after the Adam manner in the architrave and the pleasingly ingenious modification of the cornice bed-molding. No small measure of the lovely ensemble is due to the slender grace of the colonnettes supporting the complete entablature and the beautiful brass andirons and fire set.

It will be remembered that the Rev. Thomas Barnard married McIntire, and in this exquisite design and workmanship one seems to see the carver's tribute to an esteemed friend. It thrills one to stand in this room, too, realizing that this very clergyman, whose presence it so often knew, for the time being averted bloodshed during the first armed resistance to British tyranny on February 26, 1775. Dismissing his congregation at the old North Church in response to the urgent summons of a messenger, Doctor Barnard hastened to the North Bridge in the rôle of peacemaker, and finally succeeded in persuading the townspeople to lower the draw and permit the British troops to cross in their fruitless search for cannon, which, meantime, had been transferred to a new hiding place.

Returning once more to the Hosmer-Waters house, one finds in the northwest parlor an excellent Adam mantel exemplifying the combined use of carved and applied composition detail. All of the moldings are rightly of a modest nature because of the enrichment of the frieze and paneled pilasters with festoons, urns, and straight-hanging garlands. Only the bed-molding and architrave bear hand-tooling, and that of simple though effective character. This work was done in 1795 when most of the composition ornament was imported, but the American eagle never became popular with British craftsmen, and

PLATE LIV.—Mantel in the Front Parlor of the Woman's Bureau.

PLATE LV.—Detail of Mantel at the Woman's Bureau.

so McIntire himself carved the central panel in wood.

This house is of interest to the antiquary in that it was long the home of Henry FitzGilbert Waters, author of "John Harvard and His Ancestry", "An Examination into the English Ancestry of George Washington", and many papers devoted to the genealogy of prominent Salem families. His investigations in London, covering a period of several years, for the New England Historical and Genealogical Society are well known and resulted in his "Genealogical Gleanings in England." During Mr. Waters' occupancy this house contained the best private collection of rare Colonial furniture in New England.

The mantel in the west chamber of the Peabody-Silsbee house with its attractive hob-grate of ornamental iron will be seen to resemble that in the Hosmer-Waters chamber, but it is richer and shows greater refinement. A conventional cymatium replaces the rope molding with a torus and fillet separating it from the corona; the dentil course remains the same. The pilasters are reeded, and a fine-scale vertical reeded belt supplies the capitals as well as the architrave. Both the oval panel and the urns of the frieze are of composition applied.

The Wood-Carver of Salem

Reminiscent of the Lindall-Barnard-Andrews mantel, in its pairs of supporting colonnettes and corner projections of the shelf, the rear parlor mantel of the Woman's Bureau, also done in 1800, differs materially in cornice and frieze. Here again a rope molding of the utmost precision replaces the usual ovolo, and the dentil course, with its tiny triangular incisions, simulating a continuous band of guttæ from the Doric order, is without a parallel in McIntire's work. The tiny egg and dart molding beneath is in applied work, like that edging the central oval panel of the frieze, but the sheaves of wheat and the military symbolic group including a shield bearing a small eagle are of wood nicely ˆarved and glued to the face of the sunken panels. The peculiar ornamental hob-grate of cast-iron is shown with its summer blind in place.

The front parlor of the Woman's Bureau contains one of McIntire's two most fanciful mantels. The other is in the Kimball house, and both may well be considered in comparison because they are so similar yet so different and hence illustrate as few others can the resourcefulness of the one who made them. While many will say they are overornate, none can but admire the intricate carving necessary to their making, for there is no applied composition

PLATE LVI.—Detail of Mantel in the Kimball House.

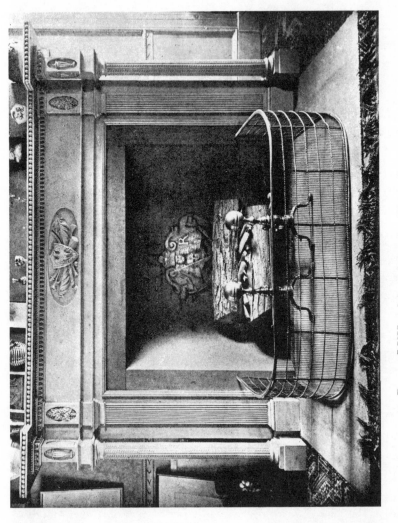

Plate LVII.—Mantel in the Kimball House.

work on either. Even the twist-drill reeds of column and cornice, the flowers and urns of the small oval inserts, and the central panels resembling one already referred to, were carved out of wood. The corner projections have been carried to the extreme in order to provide a place for flanking columns in addition to the fine-scale fluted pilasters which made it desirable, indeed necessary, to carry the shelf around the corners at each end and support it with a second pair of pilasters. But the most unique feature of all lies in the dentil course with its trumpet-like units set well apart; probably no designer before McIntire ever thought to use such a decoration on a mantel, or to insert a band of wooden spheres into the edge of a mantelshelf as in the Kimball house parlor.

This is not the only use McIntire found for a band of spheres, however; in several instances it replaced the dentil course. Employed in this manner, it appears on a large scale in the cornice of the Peabody-Silsbee house and again is to be seen in the parlor mantel of the Home for Aged Women, formerly the residence of Benjamin W. Crowninshield. Aside from the Corinthian feeling of the capitals, the design adheres to no classic order. The engaged columns are not fluted; the architrave rather than the frieze bears most of the ornament, and the cornice or mantelshelf is a thing unto itself. Yet despite its unique traits and marked unconventionality, this mantel is distinctly pleasing. Both the sheaves of wheat and the applied fruit groups in alternation with vertical reeded sections in the architrave symbolize the fullness of the harvest, motives which architects of the present day frequently make use of in country houses. Though entirely different, the beautiful surbase accords well with the architrave, while the fret of interlaced fillets at the same level about the window embrasures is one of McIntire's best and successfully fulfils his desire for variety.

As McIntire progressed in sculpture, he came to appreciate more highly its excellences and advantages for beautifying the mantel frieze, often depending almost entirely upon a horizontal bas-relief panel of stucco in which exquisitely modeled human figures were prominent. When applied to the wood and painted white, the ensemble lacked little of the daintiness and purity of marble, in those days almost prohibitive in price because of the immense amount of labor required for hand cutting.

Two notable instances of the sort occur on the third floor of the old Derby-Crowninshield-Rogers

PLATE LVIII.—Mantel in the Parlor of the Home for Aged Women.

PLATE LIX.—Parlor of the Home for Aged Women.

mansion, where, despite the shameful usage to which they have been subjected by careless tenants since the house has been devoted to commercial purposes, the mantels please the eye with their unaffected simplicity, and if cleaned and given a fresh coat of white paint would be counted among the most chaste of McIntire's work. Aside from the bas-relief panel and a conventional bed-molding above, one of these mantels boasts no ornament other than simple, hand-planed moldings, yet in several respects it finds more admirers than the other, for its very proportions render it a positive joy to look upon. The other mantel, with its detail of finer scale, implies more skilful craftsmanship because of the reeded pilasters and denticulated bed-molding. It exalts its designer no more, however, for with more ornament the effect was more easily conceived even if more laboriously executed. Indeed, it is axiomatic that the less the amount of ornament and the more the effect depends upon just proportion and carefully balanced spacing, the more difficult the task of design and the more creditable the result.

Lovely as were his mantels with sculptured friezes, McIntire is best known and most admired for his work in the Adam manner which he applied to both mantels and chimney pieces with positive genius, in several instances worthy of Robert Adam himself. Often these included a central bas-relief panel with Adam festoons at each side. Another mantel on the third floor of the old Derby-Crowninshield-Rogers house is of this character. Its structural work will be seen to resemble closely the simpler of the two mantels of this house already described. The only essential differences occur in the dentil course and the applied enrichment of the frieze, consisting of typical Adam urns, festoons, florets, and a sculptured central panel more fanciful and less pleasing than the others.

Unquestionably the finest Salem mantels done by McIntire after the Adam manner, exclusive of his chimney pieces, are those in the parlors of the David P. Waters and Clifford Crowninshield houses. The former will be seen to be an elaboration of much that has already been considered, in response to the desire for a richer effect. The cornice has been made heavier than is usually the case by the addition of a surmounting thick shelf, while the bed-molding has been augmented by the twist-drill reed above the dentil course. Used in this manner, where its cross section is not apparent, the latter has much the effect of a bead molding. The motives of the applied treatment of the frieze recall the oval panel and

PLATE LX.—Two Mantels on the Third Floor of the Derby-
Crowninshield-Rogers House.

PLATE LXI.—Corner Section of Adam Mantel, Derby-Crowninshield-Rogers House.

basket of fruits and flowers, as well as the wheat sheaves on the pilasters which were features of the Lindall-Barnard-Andrews mantel; the festoons are reminiscent of one of the Derby-Crowninshield-Rogers mantels and the reeded pilasters of another in that house. The effect here is considerably enhanced by decorating the architrave with vertical reeded groups of wood in alternation with applied rosettes, and an oval floret adorns the pilaster capital, all of which motives will be seen repeated in the surbase and cornice of the room. The photograph shows another quaint summer blind in place.

Impartial criticism seems to favor the Crowninshield mantel as representing higher refinement in design and greater precision in workmanship; certainly it is daintier, more exquisitely carved, and the applied work — festoons, urns, horns of plenty and straight-hanging garlands — are of slenderer grace. The central panel, an oval within a rectangle with its group of musical instruments, is a veritable gem, and the slight projection of the whole panel above the surface of the frieze proper lends a pleasing note of distinction. Here again the cornice has been made heavier by an additional surmounting shelf, in this instance molded on the edge with a torus between two fillets. A nicely carved bead and reel separates the cymatium from the corona, beneath which, in the rôle of a bed-molding, occurs the finest scale work of all, consisting of a band of tiny vertical flutings between ovolo and ogee moldings so tiny as to be hardly more than the smallest of reeds. Groups of flutings adorn the facings about the fireplace opening, as in the famous east parlor of the Pierce-Johonnot-Nichols house, described in the seventh chapter, and have been repeated in the surbase. Similar feeling will be noticed in the ornate cornice, which appears to be one of McIntire's welcome innovations suggested in part by the modillions of the Corinthian order and the triglyphs of the Doric.

Many, in fact most, fireplaces built about 1750 had no accompanying mantelshelf proper; although often given an architectural setting of considerable pretension, the side of the room in which they occurred sometimes was entirely paneled up with ornamental molded facings about the fireplace opening. The desire for, almost the need of, this pleasing and useful adjunct probably accounts for the several McIntire mantels put into old houses, some of which were erected before his birth. Two such instances at "The Lindens", Danvers, erected in 1745, and referred to in the third chapter, are shown by accompanying illustrations.

PLATE LXII.—Detail of Mantel in the
David P. Waters Reception Room.

PLATE LXIII.—Parlor of the Clifford Crowninshield House.

Mantels and Chimney Pieces

Taken from the Nathan Read house, designed by McIntire in 1790 and referred to in the third chapter, these mantels are seen at a glance not to have been built for their present locations. Although their height is such as to split the lowest of three original horizontal panels, McIntire was not responsible for this blunder, nor is it serious enough to detract greatly from the beauty of the mantels themselves, particularly in the instance where a handsome gilt Adam mirror virtually conceals it. In both instances the slight projection of the paneling and cornice over the fireplace combine with the mantel to simulate the effect of a complete chimney piece.

The frieze of one of these mantels recalls that of the David P. Waters parlor mantel, without the festoons of the latter and including a simpler architrave, consisting of a continuous band of exceedingly fine vertical reedings. The broad, reeded pilasters are heavier and the Corinthian capitals are not present in the Waters mantel, while the broad molded facings about the fireplace opening are by no means common to Salem architecture.

Rarely did McIntire's work take such a light and fanciful character as in the other mantel at "The Lindens." The bed-molding is a repetition of that of the Peabody-Silsbee mantel, and the twist-drill motive also appears again here. In fact, the latter provides a prominent repeated theme in the cornice, the architrave, and the narrow paneled pilasters. A broad Grecian fret of well-known pattern supplies the architrave and sounds an unusual note in McIntire design, but chief interest centers in the applied work, not so much in the central panel as in the horns of plenty which serve as frieze spots at each side and particularly the realistic grapevines and fruit which replace the conventional Adam garlands in the paneled pilasters. Although perhaps attracting too much attention to themselves, the pictorial Flemish tiles are of peculiar interest as antiques.

With due respect to McIntire's resourcefulness and good taste, his rare versatility, and remarkable success in the design of varied architectural features, his complete chimney pieces must be regarded as surpassing all his other achievements. In conceiving them he may be said veritably to have outdone himself; certainly no century-old chimney pieces in America equal them in harmonious ensemble, subtle proportion, or exquisite detail; they are in every way superlative. While the mantels themselves closely resemble those already described, they are richer in ornament throughout, and with the

PLATE LXIV.—Detail of Mantel in the Clifford Crowninshield
Parlor.

PLATE LXV.—Two Chimney Pieces at "The Lindens," Danvers.

Mantels and Chimney Pieces

elaboration of the upper part of the chimney breast or overmantel into a highly decorative frame for a mirror or the family portrait take on much greater dignity and pretension.

Although the chimney piece in the east parlor of the Pierce-Johonnot-Nichols house, illustrated and described in the seventh chapter, is best known, no house contains so many or such beautiful examples as "Oak Hill", Peabody, to which frequent reference was made in the fourth chapter. All are after the Adam manner and savor of the Corinthian order, yet differ considerably in detail, although in each one notices the repeated use of McIntire's favorite double denticulated and vertical reeded ovolo moldings. By extending the cornice and frieze around the chimney breast and carrying a pilaster effect up through them, they have been made virtually a part of the chimney piece and a means to relate it closely to the architectural setting of the entire room. As a whole, the effect of each is one of delightful harmony, chaste elegance, and graceful dignity.

Critical examination of the chimney pieces in the drawing-room and chamber discloses many characteristics in common. In both, variety with complete harmony avoids monotony and preserves good taste. Reeded pilasters or engaged columns support the mantelshelf, while paneled pilasters with beautiful applied work are employed for the overmantel, the horns of plenty on those of the drawing-room being unusual. Beautiful composition moldings frame the square panel of the overmantel, scroll and acanthus flower patterns being used together in one, and the pattern of alternate florets and reeded groups being employed with the scroll in the other, thus putting this drawing-room overmantel frame in pleasing accord with the frieze of the room. The flower vases of the chamber mantel frieze contribute a new note, as do the grape clusters in the drawing-room and the use of the baskets of fruit and flowers each side of a pastoral bas-relief panel in the center. In both instances reminiscent of the Cook-Oliver parlor mantel, illustrated in the sixth chapter, the acanthus leaf applied to the cymatium of the mantel-shelf greatly enriches the effect, while the marble facings of the fireplace opening, both the plain slabs in the chamber and those magnificently incised with a Grecian fret in the drawing-room, preserve the chaste appearance so essential to the purity of the fireplace in the unavoidable transition from structural wood to structural stone.

Architects regard this drawing-room chimney piece as one of McIntire's greatest works, yet fine as

PLATE LXVI.—Chimney Piece in the Drawing-Room, "Oak Hill."

PLATE LXVII.—Corner Section of Drawing-Room Mantel, "Oak Hill."

PLATE LXVIII.—Chimney Piece in the Morning Room, "Oak Hill."

PLATE LXIX.—Chimney Piece in a Chamber at "Oak Hill."

it is, the less spectacular chimney piece in the morning room excels it in harmony of line; it is a veritable symphony of vertical reeding, conservative in applied ornament yet rich in effect by reason of its fine scale and precision of workmanship. Unlike any other, this distinctive piece of work will be remembered for its reserve, refinement, and effective simplicity. Here, as well as in the other fireplaces at "Oak Hill", the handsome brass andirons and fire-set form an interesting study.

CHAPTER VI

THE COOK–OLIVER HOUSE

UNFORTUNATELY for the antiquary and the architect, the largest and handsomest dwelling designed by McIntire no longer exists in its entirety. Happily, however, the plans and a picture of it have been preserved, and much of the splendid woodwork taken from it was built into another house, still standing in an excellent state of preservation at Number 142 Federal Street. Whereas certain Salem buildings erected during that notable period from 1782 to 1811 command attention chiefly for architectural excellence, others for historic association, this so-called Cook-Oliver house combines the two in rare degree and possesses the additional attraction of being very closely associated with the chief source of Salem's prosperity.

A stately mansion, standing in the shade of splendid old trees, it still compares favorably with anything old or new in Salem; but even were it hidden from view, the very gateposts would attract and

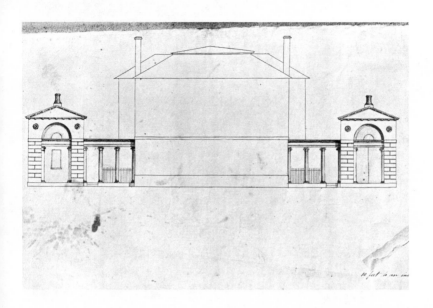

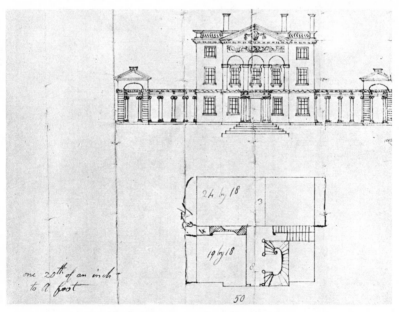

PLATE LXX.—Preliminary Sketches, Elias Haskett Derby Mansion.

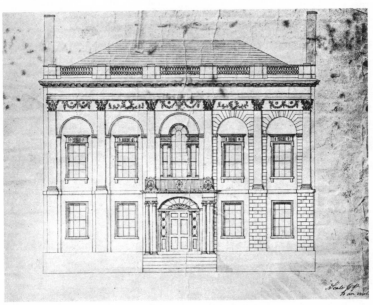

PLATE LXXI.—Preliminary Front Elevations, Elias Haskett
Derby Mansion.

hold the attention of any intelligent passer-by, so chaste and beautiful is their design. They are the work of Samuel McIntire, who hand tooled them in 1799 to adorn the entrance of the Elias Haskett Derby mansion, where they were first erected. Derby, who was Salem's greatest merchant and prominent in the equipment of privateers during the Revolution, spent eighty thousand dollars on the house, which was said to be the most sumptuous in America at that time and gave McIntire the opportunity for his greatest achievement as an architect of domestic buildings. It stood between Essex and Front Streets, on what had formerly been the Colonel William Brown estate, the grounds extending to the water's edge and being beautifully laid out and terraced. The second edition of Felt's "Annals of Salem" contains a picture of it, reproduced on another page, and McIntire's own plans, also reproduced and showing the gradual development from preliminary drawings, may be seen at the Essex Institute.

The Derby gardens, famous throughout New England, owed their beauty chiefly to the good taste and superior knowledge of George Heussler, an Alsatian, the first professional gardener in the vicinity, who came to this country from Harlaam and Am-

sterdam in 1780, bringing diplomas and recommenda-
tions. His horticultural pursuits were begun in the
employ of John Tracy of Newburyport, where he
married. In 1790, owing to Tracy's financial diffi-
culties, Heussler moved to Salem and continued
to work at his chosen vocation at the town residence
and also at the farm of Elias Haskett Derby in that
part of Danvers now known as Peabody. To his
influence is due in large measure the exceptional attention which persons of wealth throughout Essex
County gave to their gardens, and to him must be
attributed the credit for introducing many flowers
and valuable fruits new to America.

Reverend William Bentley in his famous diary,
under date of October 24, 1801, describes a visit to
the farm, then occupied by Derby's son, and refers
particularly to the exotic flowers, the oranges, lemons,
and other rare fruits which he saw in the green-
houses. The beautiful summer or teahouse, formerly
another important architectural feature of this
garden, and now congenially located in a neighboring town, presents one of McIntire's most delightful
and effective classic adaptations, while the urns at
the four corners of the roof and particularly the
figure of a reaper with his scythe carved in wood
and standing at one end may be regarded as among

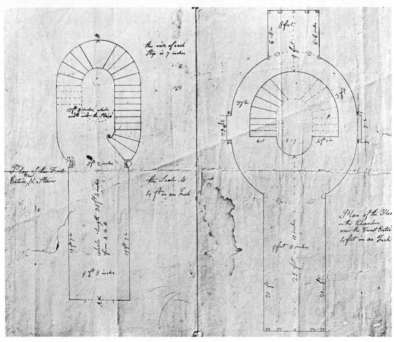

PLATE LXXII.—Woodcut of the Elias Haskett Derby Mansion from Felt's "Annals of Salem"; Floor Plans of the Stair Hall.

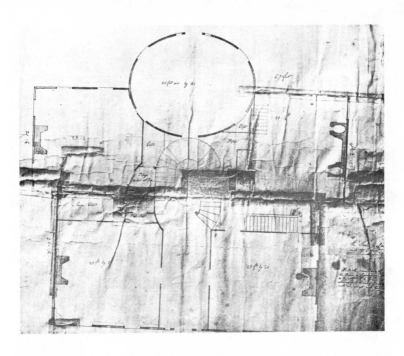

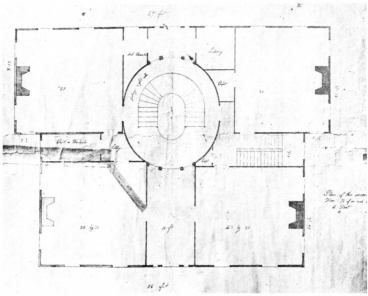

PLATE LXXIII.—First and Second Floor Plans, Elias Haskett
Derby Mansion.

his most ambitious successes in sculpture. At the opposite end of the roof there also stood formerly the figure of a milkmaid, like its companion representing an important farm industry and so symbolizing the spirit of agriculture. The whole structure is exceptional in its elongated rectangular shape and just proportions, the beautiful pediment, supporting pilasters and window frames, taking the form of the Ionic order and providing adornment of a refined and suitable character. Within, a stairway leads to the second floor, where one finds a surprisingly beautiful room with coved ceiling, paneled wainscot, and charming built-in cupboards for those dainty things pertaining to afternoon tea.

It is interesting to recall that Derby was the first American merchant to open trade with the Cape of Good Hope in 1784 and with China the following year. To those far-off shores he sent the famous *Grand Turk*, a fast sailing-ship of three hundred tons which originally had been built for him as a privateer. A painting of it in a large punch bowl, made at Canton, China, in 1786, may be seen in the Peabody Museum. Later, in 1788, Derby's ship *Atlantic* opened the East India trade, being the first to carry the American ensign into the harbors of Bombay and Calcutta.

The Wood-Carver of Salem

Upon Derby's death, only a few months after he moved into his new home from the Pickman-Derby-Brookhouse estate at the corner of Washington and Lynde Streets, which he had formerly occupied, the mansion was closed. No purchaser could be found for so expensive an establishment, and so in 1804 the gateposts and much of the charming wood finish, including some of the best examples of McIntire's genius in design, were removed and built into the new residence then being erected under McIntire's direction for Captain Samuel Cook, a master mariner whose silhouette portrait may be seen at the Essex Institute. Later, in 1815, the Derby mansion was completely torn down, and the land on which it stood was given by the heirs to the town for a permanent market, ever since known as Derby Square.

The story goes that just before leaving on a long voyage Captain Cook approved McIntire's design and gave him the commission to have the house erected under his direction. The trip proved so unsuccessful, however, that upon his return Captain Cook despaired of being able to complete the undertaking and ordered the work stopped. But McIntire, with all the self-sacrificing enthusiasm of the builders of old, expressed his eagerness to go

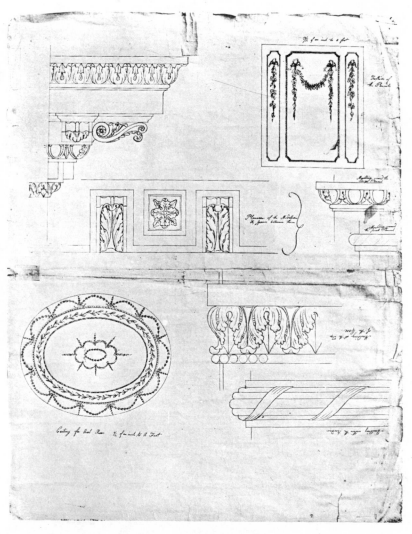

PLATE LXXIV.—Detail of Carved Moldings and Stucco Work, Elias Haskett Derby Mansion.

PLATE LXXV.—Plan of Garden and Grounds, Elias Haskett Derby Mansion.

ahead with it slowly, as his associates had spare time, payment to be made accordingly. Moreover, in prevailing upon Captain Cook to buy considerable of the fine woodwork then being taken out of the Derby mansion he not only saved his client considerable expense but at a single stroke transformed what had originally been intended as only an ordinary house into one of rare charm and distinction, and also preserved several of his greatest achievements intact to posterity. Thus the Cook house was from eight to eleven years in the building. McIntire did not live to see all of the interiors completed, but his plans were executed by his brother Joseph, who had regularly been associated with him as a housewright and master builder, and for the most part the work was done with material which had been prepared before his death.

In more recent times the Cook house was occupied until his death in 1885 by Captain Cook's son-in-law, General Henry Kemble Oliver, the famous composer and musician. Here he married Sally Cook and wrote several of his well-known church hymns, including "Federal Street", so dear to the hearts of all Salem residents. His was a life of varied and useful service, since he was at different times one of the early mayors of Lawrence, treasurer of her great cotton mills, Adjutant General and State Treasurer of Massachusetts, and Mayor of Salem in his eightieth year.

A study of the Cook-Oliver house ensemble indicates clearly that McIntire rightly regarded the fence as a purely architectural feature which should accord with the house. His pickets, rails, and bases were always of extreme simplicity, with some interesting departure from continued verticality in the gate, as seen here, and considerable elaboration of the gateposts, often, as in this instance, four in number in front of the house, with simpler posts for any continuation of the fence and a simpler gateway for the side entrance. These high, square gateposts with their shapely urns and surmounting flame motives are the best and most elaborate of the many in Salem by McIntire.

They consist of a base, paneled shaft, and entablature, the shaft panels containing beautifully carved, straight-hanging garlands, and the frieze panels containing oval sunburst medallions. The fine-scale cornice included a vertical-fluted belt similar to the much heavier one across the front of the house at the second-floor level. Another repetition to relate house and fence and to brighten the whole effect is that of the straight-hanging garlands,

PLATE LXXVI.—The Cook-Oliver House, erected in 1804.

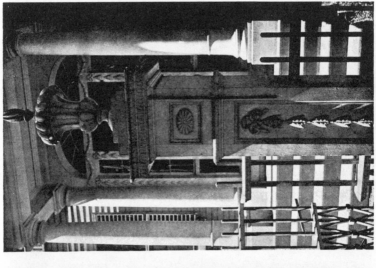

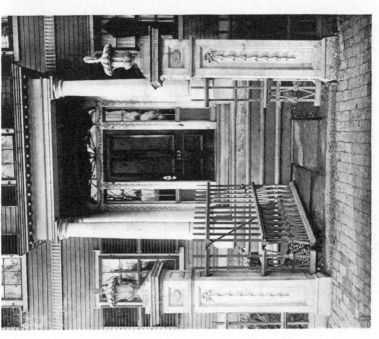

PLATE LXXVII.—Detail of Cook-Oliver Gateway and Porch; Detail of Gatepost.

one of which decorates each of the vertical door casings, while a festooned garland stretches across the head. These garlands, favorite motives of the brothers Adam, indicate positively their influence upon McIntire's work and account in large measure for its refinement.

Conforming to the prevailing style of that period, the Cook-Oliver house is a white-painted, square structure, three stories high, with a two-story ell, the third story of the main house being foreshortened with almost square, nine-paned windows to reduce the apparent total height. All the other windows have twelve-paned Georgian sashes which with their two-part green blinds range absolutely on all elevations. Clapboards cover the walls with rather narrow exposure to the weather, except for the eastern side of the main house, which is of brick, affording, before its neighbor was built, greater protection against the northeast storms off the sea. Several Salem houses are constructed in this manner. The low hip roof is shingled, and like many houses built for seafaring men of Salem and other New England seaport towns was originally decked with a surrounding balustrade and reached through a scuttle.

Severity of line in the whole house is relieved by several decorative features of pleasing and refined appearance. A heavy cornice with large molded dentils adorns the eaves. The second-story windows are elaborated by the addition of beautiful entablatures above the heads, the simple window casings of architrave motive being exactly like those on both other floors. These entablatures are hand carved in fine-scale detail with denticulated cornice moldings supported by a flat pilaster effect each side of the frieze, the latter consisting of a central horizontal band, vertical-fluted, flanked by an oval medallion beside each pilaster. At the level of the second floor and porch cornice a broad horizontal belt of vertical-fluted wood finish extends across the entire façade, seeming in a sense to "tie" the porch to the house.

Most important of the exterior decorative features are the porch and doorway, showing individuality in design and a keen sense of harmony in adaptation. Upon these McIntire focused the full measure of his skill, as was the custom of the time, with the result that they stand out with exceptional grace, repose, and dignity, even among the many notable examples in Salem. The naïve manner in which free use was made of the orders, characteristic of much of his work, and the surprising harmony, charm of line, and proportion, achieved with such absence of restraint,

PLATE LXXVIII.—Cook-Oliver Entrance, showing Window Heads.

PLATE LXXIX.—Stairway, Cook-Oliver House.

furnish eloquent tribute to McIntire's keen discrimination and artistic perception. In the face of such evidence it cannot be said that "the architect of Salem" was any mere copyist.

The porch of the Cook-Oliver house is entirely of wood, including the steps; substantial but distinctly inviting. The columns, with their smooth shafts and high, square plinths, both those at the front and also the engaged columns each side of the doorway, suggest the Tuscan rather more than the Roman Doric, while the entablature seems to be an Ionic adaptation with flat, plain frieze and denticulated cornice. An elliptical fanlight and vertical side lights, all subdivided with exceptional grace, contain the original Colonial glass, and it is interesting to remember that quite aside from the beauty of these sashes the difficulty of making large sheets of glass and its consequent high cost in those days were partial reasons for adopting them. The same was true of ordinary windows, though the subdivisions were useful to give scale, and it is as much for that purpose that they are so much used to-day as to carry out any period adaptation. Two-part green blinds, characteristic of the time and the predecessor of the modern screen door, are hung outside the paneled wooden door.

The Wood-Carver of Salem

In such a house it is natural to expect great refinement of the interior woodwork, and one is not disappointed. White pine, so easily worked and so enduring, was used exclusively. It is painted white, carved and molded in a masterly manner. As in many old houses of the time, the hall extends directly through to the rear of the house, whence a door opens upon a picturesque garden. At the left-hand side of the hall a flight of stairs rises to the second floor, broken three steps below the top by a landing where the direction of the run reverses. Delightful in its slender grace, the balustrade consists of a molded rail and simple turned newel and balusters. A Palladian window on the landing lights the stairway, and at the head of the lower run stands a "clock on the stairs", recalling Longfellow's immortal poem. A flat wainscot with its molded base and surbase hand-carved in fine-scale, vertical-reeded motive extends up the wall side of the stairway, and the stair ends are decorated by a sort of double scroll jig-sawed out of lumber somewhat less than an inch in thickness and applied to the wood trim over the stair stringer.

Most of the casings throughout the house are molded after the manner of an architrave, but those in the hall, which were taken from the Derby

PLATE LXXX.—Doorway in Cook-Oliver Hall.

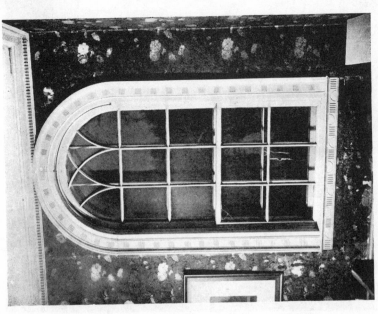

Plate LXXXI.—Palladian Window, Cook-Oliver Hall; Corner Section of Hall Door.

mansion, are exquisitely hand-carved and otherwise decorated with applied ornament, demonstrating the refined and subtle effect of straight lines relieved by curves only in the trim of the head. There
is at once harmony and great variety in the combined
use of both vertical and horizontal cuttings, the
flutings and reedings being almost perfect in execution. Salem has no more exquisite examples of
interior wood finish than these heads with their
gracefully festooned draperies, fruit-filled urns, and
rosettes. The cornice has one deeply-carved molding, and the same motive, resembling a double dentil
and a favorite with McIntire, is repeated in a cornice
molding about the ceiling of the hall. One notices
with pleasure, also, the panel arrangement of the
door, the brass-mounted glass knob, and the brass
key-plate.

The accompanying photographs of the hall illustrate well a beautiful, old, imported wall paper that
appears to be unmatched in America. It was hand
blocked in eighteen-inch squares and consists of pink
roses on a background of green leaves, the coloring
having been softened and improved by the passage
of time. Owing to its unique character, the paper
was purchased early this year by the Metropolitan
Museum of Art and has since been removed, cleaned,

and taken to New York, where it will adorn one of the several Colonial rooms to become an important, permanent feature of the Museum. Antiquaries may regret its removal from the house where it was first hung, but better certain preservation in this way than possible ruin by some unsympathetic owner of the future.

Through one of the hall doorways can be seen a glimpse of the parlor with its splendid mantel and French scenic wall paper, brought from Europe by Captain Cook about 1820 on his return from one of his sea voyages. It is said that he bought the paper to decorate the "best room" for the approaching marriage of his daughter to General Henry Kemble Oliver in 1825. This quaint wall paper was probably printed by J. Zuber & Company, a famous old Alsatian firm, and its grays, greens, and black with touches of red and yellow have become delightfully mellow with age. It depicts the panorama of Paris as viewed from the Seine a century ago, and includes much of interest to the antiquary. Several panels now show the ravages of time somewhat, yet it is to be hoped that the present owner will preserve them intact. The west wall, representing a pastoral scene, remains virtually as perfect as ever and is among the most beautiful specimens of old hand-

PLATE LXXXII.—Parlor Mantel and Scenic Wall Paper, Cook-
Oliver House; Corner Section of Mantel.

PLATE LXXXIII.—Wall of Parlor, Cook-Oliver House, showing "Panorama of Paris" Wall Paper; Embrasured Windows with Folding Shutters.

blocked wall paper to be found anywhere. Tradition tells us that General Oliver composed "Federal
Street" and several other well-known hymns in this
room.

Delicate in design and superbly executed, few
Salem mantels equal that in the parlor of the Cook-
Oliver house. It was hand-carved by McIntire, in
1799, for the Derby mansion, and among other features was removed to its present location. Daintier
moldings it would be difficult to conceive; the classic
acanthus leaf of the top cyma molding, as well as of
the smaller molding below the frieze spot, and the
familiar tiny bead molding are prominent, yet there is
a certain ingenuousness in their use, and particularly
so in the application of the acanthus leaf to the capitals of the two slender, reeded colonnettes.

A flat, unadorned central panel with nicely delineated medallions on each of the pilasters provides the
distinctive but somewhat meager decoration of the
frieze, while the architrave repeats the festooned
garland effect seen elsewhere indoors and out.
Doubtless the central panel originally contained
some form of applied ornament after the characteristic McIntire manner. The acanthus leaves, bead
molding, medallions, and garland decorations are
good examples of appropriate applied ornament.

By no means the least interesting feature of this fireplace is the beautiful brass hob-grate set in soapstone, the first of its kind ever placed in a Salem house and at that time considered a great extravagance. Indeed, in nearly all the fireplaces of the house there are grates rather than hearths. A surbase extending about the room above the flat dado, hand-tooled in 1804 when the house was built, displays a delicate incised pattern consisting of two entwined bands or fillets, one a flat ribbon and the other made up of repeated round discs. It suggests a modification of the lozenge fret with segmental sides. At the embrasured windows five-part paneled shutters fold into side pockets in such a way that they carry upward the panel effect of the wainscot below.

The dining room, at the left of the front door, reflects the parlor, but is simpler in treatment, especially the mantel. On the floors above, large, nearly square rooms open off the hall at each side. Architecturally they are notable chiefly for their simple, well-proportioned mantels and modest, fine-scale cornices. The ell includes a large kitchen and laundry, with servants' rooms above.

PLATE LXXXIV.—Detail of Parlor Mantel, Cook-Oliver House.

Plate LXXXV.—The Dining Room, Cook-Oliver House.

PLATE LXXXVI.—Detail of Mantel in Chamber over Parlor.

PLATE LXXXVII.—Chamber over Dining Room, Cook-Oliver House.

CHAPTER VII

THE PIERCE–JOHONNOT–NICHOLS HOUSE

O F Salem's many splendid old mansions, the Pierce-Johonnot-Nichols house, Number 80 Federal Street, has generally come to be regarded as the architectural gem, the finest wooden house in New England, and also the principal monument to the genius of Samuel McIntire now in existence. While it boasts no direct association with persons or events of great national importance, over this imposing residence the pathos of financial adversity and a romantic friendship sheds a golden glow.

In the planning, and later in the building of the house and development of the grounds, this estate was the pride and joy of Jerathmel Pierce, a wealthy East India merchant. Here were centered virtually his every life-interest both in home and in business. At the rear the land sloped away to a wharf and warehouse on the North River, then a navigable stream, to which his ships came heavy laden with fragrant spices and beautiful fabrics. The intervening space, through which he passed and repassed daily, was handsomely laid out as a terraced and formal garden, with box-bordered paths, stone steps, and picturesque wooden arches, fruit trees, and a wealth of flowers. Many leisure hours were spent directing the yearly improvements, and with his own hands much tender care was bestowed upon his friends of the horticultural world; it was his recreation and his exercise. So well was the work done that even to-day what remains of the old garden retains much of its pristine charm, although the warehouse at its western end no longer remains, and successive embankments have gradually encroached upon the river until it now resembles a mere canal at this point. No home lover can fail to understand how completely this estate became an expression of the joys, successes, and aspirations of its owner.

For forty-four years this ideal condition continued, and then came disaster. Ventures at sea are precarious at best, the Embargo and Non-Intercourse Acts had imposed great hardships upon New England merchants, and in 1826 both Jerathmel Pierce and his son-in-law, George Nichols, lost their fortunes. In consequence it became necessary the following year for the older man to give up his most cherished

Plate LXXXVIII.—Detail of Mantel in Chamber over Dining Room, Cook-Oliver House.

PLATE LXXXIX.—The Pierce-Johonnot-Nichols House, erected in 1782.

possession, his home, which was bought by George Johonnot, an old friend of both families. Jerathmel Pierce, then in his eightieth year, could not bear the shock of so great a change in his life and circumstances; only once after going to live with his son-in-law in the famous old Tontine Block, formerly on Warren Street, did he venture to look at the stately home which had once been his, and shortly afterward he died broken-hearted.

Later, in 1840, when both Mr. and Mrs. Johonnot also died within a month of each other, it was discovered that the house had been bequeathed to George Nichols and his wife to be held in trust during their lives for their four daughters, who were eventually to inherit it outright. And thus through a remarkable bond of friendship, the property was restored to the descendants of him who had created and loved it so dearly, and the son-in-law was enabled to pass his declining years in the house where he married his first wife and where his second wife, Betsey Pierce, was born. What a benevolent tribute to the sacrifice of a friend, the greatness of which George Johonnot came to realize more fully through living on this delightful estate and experiencing an ever growing fondness for it himself! Is it to be wondered at that lovers of romance and of good

architecture alike rejoice in the fact that the Essex
Institute is raising a fund with which to purchase and
perpetuate the estate in as nearly its original condition as possible ? An effort will also be made to
reassemble the large and excellent collection of
antique furniture, rare china, and silver.

Among the other square houses of Salem, this
fine old residence stands architecturally unique and
distinct. Like the Cook-Oliver house, it was many
years in the building, for those were the days of
thorough workmanship, and without machinery of
any sort for the manufacture of either structural
lumber or wood trim, the preparation of the material
was in itself a slow and expensive matter. Erected
in 1782, it was not completed until 1800. In this
fact lies the source of its greatest charm, for the
western half is purely Georgian in conception,
whereas the eastern half, built eighteen years later,
obviously reflects Adam influence throughout, and
so in a single house constitutes to a certain degree
a record of the development of McIntire's mind
toward a style of greater delicacy and refinement.

Exteriorly this is particularly true of the picturesque one-story portion along one side of the brick-
paved stable courtyard, its series of broad doors under
elliptical fanlights somewhat after the manner of a

PLATE XC.—Detail of Gateway and Porch, Pierce-Johonnot-Nichols House.

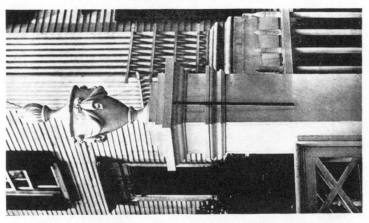

PLATE XCI.—Detail of Corner Treatment, Pierce-Johonnot-Nichols House; Hand carved Eagle on Barn Roof; Detail of hand carved Gatepost.

colonnade and in their treatment utterly at variance with the severity of the front and side entrances. On the opposite side of this courtyard and across one end range the stable and various outbuildings, through one of which the stairway leading down into the garden is reached. Likewise elaborated by a clever adaptation of the flat elliptical arch, these buildings together with the adjacent side of the house form a picture redolent of the quaint New England spirit equal to any stage-setting ever conceived by David Belasco from Salem inspiration. On the roof of one of these outbuildings still roosts in an excellent state of preservation one of McIntire's famous wooden eagles. They were popular then and much used in connection with domestic as well as public work, for those were times when the eagle as a symbol of Americanism meant much and was close to the heart of every true patriot.

As a whole the greater depth, breadth, and foreshortened third story of the Pierce-Johonnot-Nichols house give it a mass much more pleasing than the average square Salem house. Its unique distinction, however, lies in the attractive balustrades of the low, hip roof and belvedere, whence arriving ships might be watched for, and the welcome embellishment of the fluted pilaster treatment at the corners, a free use of the Doric order, which goes a long way in mitigating the severity in shape of a square house. The Doric spirit also pervades the entrance porch at the front and the enclosed porch at the side doorway, that early forerunner of the modern vestibule. No better instances of pleasing proportion and delicate detail are to be found in New England. Despite the fact that Doric, severest of the orders, is better suited to public than domestic work unless interpreted with the utmost sympathy, and notwithstanding the unresponsiveness of a solid wood door without side lights, which were rarely found in houses prior to 1800, McIntire succeeded in imparting to these doorways a certain indefinable quality of dignified individuality tempered by the characteristic Salem breadth which makes them friendly doorways; they speak of a genuine welcome beyond these conventional barriers of seeming reserve. One sees clearly here that gateways and doorways are closely allied; in fact, are virtually parts of the same effect when treated in harmony, providing an architectural setting for the vista of the doorway itself between them.

The window treatment, both of heads and casings, is one of effective simplicity, and the dark-painted doors with panels well spaced are equipped with

PLATE XCII.—Enclosed Side Porch, Pierce-Johonnot-Nichols House.

PLATE XCIII.—Old Terraced Garden, Pierce-Johonnot-Nichols Estate.

PLATE XCIV.—Paved Courtyard between Pierce-Johonnot-
Nichols House and Barn, from two viewpoints.

PLATE XCV.—Hall and Stairway, Pierce-Johonnot-Nichols House; Detail of Chippendale Balustrade.

quaint brass hardware, including one of the best knockers in Salem.

Praiseworthy as is the exterior design of this noble example of Colonial architecture, its interior adornment evokes the unrestrained admiration of all, for here in his later capacity of architect and designer McIntire found ample opportunity to employ the product of his original vocation of wood-carver. Upon entering the hall the stairway at once commands attention, its unusual balustrade, as well as the fret along the second-floor level, undoubtedly owing its origin to Chippendale influence. Four slender square balusters alternate with a jig-sawed member very like the well-known chair back to form a scheme at once unique and beautiful. Chippendale's work preceded that of Adam; already occasional examples of his splendid craftsmanship were being brought to America, and it followed naturally that McIntire, in his search for distinctive motives for the interior of this house at the time of its inception, came as completely under the spell of Chippendale as he did later that of Adam.

After the manner of the time jig-sawed double scrolls decorate the stair ends, in this instance also bearing three pairs of vertical flutes which sound the only false note of consequence in the entire house.

The Wood-Carver of Salem

The ingenious newel treatment suggests the volute
of the Ionic order, the balustrade with its square
balusters winding scroll fashion about a simple
turned column and the first stair tread taking the
outline of the rail above.

Other features of interest in the hall include the
hand-tooled denticulated molding of the cornice with
a bead and dentil in alternation, each dentil having
a flute carefully gouged upon it; the vertical fluted
surbase of the wainscot; the beautiful Palladian
window on the landing three steps below the top
of the stairway, where the direction of the run reverses, and the approach from the landing by two
semicircular steps to a door opening upon a chamber
at the rear of the house. One looks backward, too,
with admiration toward the inside of the front doorway and fanlight which have been elaborated considerably in rare good taste. Here may be studied
one of those instances of delightful proportion which,
as much as the design and exceptional workmanship,
have rendered Salem architecture superior to much
contemporaneous work elsewhere. The casings with
their broad horizontal flutings below the Corinthian
capitals sound an unusual though pleasing note, as
do the beaded panels with urn-shaped inserts in applied work each side of the fanlight. The ornamenta-

PLATE XCVI.—Second Floor Hall, Pierce-Johonnot-Nichols House;
Third Floor Hall.

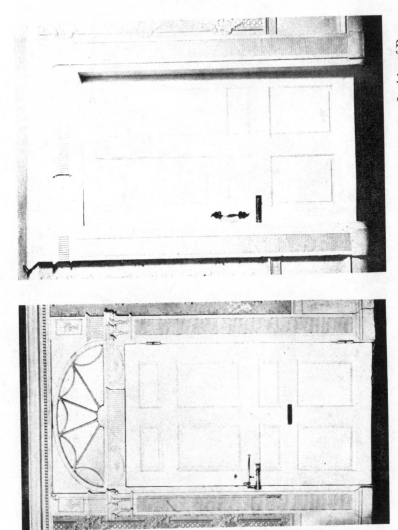

PLATE XCVII.—Inside of Front Door, Pierce-Johonnot-Nichols House; Inside of Rear Door.

PLATE XCIX.—West or Georgian Parlor, Pierce-Johonnot-Nichols House; Doorway and Architectural Treatment.

tion of the lintel with festoons and rosettes each side of a vertical reeded central panel, however, exemplifies a typical Adam treatment. A comparison of this with the simpler though similar rear door under the stairway landing will prove interesting.

The east and west parlors contain the best examples of McIntire's creative talent as a designer. The latter, a room sixteen and one half feet square, was finished in 1782 along Georgian though hardly conventional lines, for it has individuality; more, the wood finish here as throughout the house evinces that superlative skill in the use of plane and chisel which indisputably placed McIntire among our foremost early craftsmen. Decidedly substantial in character, it is essentially simple in conception and graceful in form and proportion. A flat dado with molded base and surbase, also a heavy cornice, surround the room and serve to combine its several features into a unified whole. First attention naturally goes to the fireplace and its treatment, which here, as in many old houses, has been made part of one side of the room architecturally treated with wood paneling throughout. Upon chimney pieces McIntire ever focused his greatest skill, because of their importance as centers of home life, with the result that they stand out with exceptional beauty of proportion and refinement of detail. The precision and regularity of repetition in the incised moldings cannot but evoke unstinted praise, the more so considering the laborious manner in which they had to be tooled by hand.

Of these moldings the ovolo under the shelf will be seen to be a repetition of that in the cornice above the dentil course. Generally speaking, an interpretation of the classic egg and tongue motive, it was employed without the customary bead and reel and still further received the stamp of McIntire's personality by the small round borings at the base of the tongue. A related but dissimilar ovolo molding surrounds the broad panel of the overmantel, while the ogee moldings about the fireplace opening but faintly resemble any well-known ancient motive, though restrained and effective. Thus McIntire varied and recombined classic detail, nor did his creative instinct permit him again and again to copy these motives mechanically, but rather induced him to freshen them here and there with innovations of his own which indicate clearly his native ingenuity and keen sense of the fitness of things.

The beautiful brass hob-grate mounted on soapstone recalls a similar one in the Cook-Oliver house and compares favorably with any in America, its

PLATE C.—Embrasured Windows and Seats, West Parlor, Pierce-
Johonnot-Nichols House; Detail of Mantel.

PLATE CI.—Detail of Chimney Piece and China Closet, West Parlor, Pierce-Johonnot-Nichols House; Corner Section of the Mantel.

PLATE CII.—Detail of Embrasured Window and Seat, West Parlor,
Pierce-Johonnot-Nichols House.

PLATE CIII.—General View of East or Adam Parlor, Pierce-Johonnot-Nichols House.

setting within a border of blue and white tiles which depict animals in the wild and hunting scenes being exceptional.

Both the doors and windows of this room deserve careful scrutiny, the former for the arrangement of their molded panels, the casings or architrave motive, their striking caps, and the delightfully quaint hardware, particularly the brass drop handles. Were it not established otherwise, the old wrought-iron strap hinges would indicate positively the early origin of the work. The quarter-circular ends of the frieze board above the lintel lend a distinct touch of individuality, as does also the square-end finish board above, which ties the doorhead into the cornice corresponding to the treatment of the windows. The latter, twelve-paned in accordance with the best Salem custom, it will be noticed, are deeply embrasured with seats underneath and paneled shutters folding into side pockets.

It is the east parlor, however, which has become a veritable Mecca for architects from all sections of the country. Done in 1800 at a time when McIntire had yielded completely to the spell of those master craftsmen of England, America has no contemporaneous example of the Adam influence superior to this very room. In size a veritable drawing-room sixteen and one half by twenty-six and one half feet, it possesses the spaciousness which alone emphasizes to the full that subtle quality of nice balance between the plain surfaces and delicate ornament to which the Adam manner owes its principal charm of refinement. Indeed, the flat dado with its molded surbase embellished with groups of vertical flutings, the pilaster treatment of the corners with Corinthian capital and fluted shaft resting on an appropriate pedestal, the heavy cornice with delicately carved moldings and frieze with rosettes and vertical reeded groups in alternation on a flat ground, the embrasured windows with hand-tooled casings and paneled shutters, and last, but best of all, the magnificent chimney piece, provide an architectural setting of rare beauty for some fine old furniture, paintings, and bric-a-brac long cherished by the family.

A favorite McIntire motive, ever recurring with minor variations throughout his work in the Adam manner, occupies the stringcourse of the cornice. This double dentil or Grecian fret is formed by vertical cross-cuttings alternately from the top and bottom of a square molding, the fine-scale reeded ovolo beneath giving it just the right emphasis and relating the cornice as a whole more closely to the ornamentation of the frieze. On the under surface

PLATE CIV.—Front and Rear Ends East or Adam Parlor, Pierce-Johonnot-Nichols House.

PLATE CV.—Detail of Doorway, East Parlor, Pierce-Johonnot-Nichols House.

PLATE CVI.—Detail of Adam Chimney Piece, East Parlor,
Pierce-Johonnot-Nichols House.

PLATE CVII.—Corner Section of East Parlor Mantel, Pierce-Johonnot-Nichols House.

of the projecting cornice and frieze another fret, consisting of interlacing circular fillets, large and small circles in alternation with applied rosettes within the larger ones, represents considerable painstaking effort.

Turning to the chimney piece, unquestionably the finest in Salem, the logical manner in which both cornice and frieze have been carried about and made a part of it, thus tying it into the entire scheme, at once elicits hearty commendation. Delicate handplaned moldings which echo the motives prominent elsewhere in the room do much toward beautifying this chimney piece, notably the reeded pilasters, the fluted band about the fireplace opening, and the dentil course under the shelf which McIntire elaborated somewhat by cutting into the surface of each dentil with a gouge. The pilasters above the shelf, the molding surrounding the large panel over the chimney breast, in which a mirror or painting was usually set, as, in this instance, the corona of the shelf, which is in itself another cornice, and the capitals of the reeded pilasters each side of the fireplace opening, all display exquisite applied work. The ornamentation of the mantelboard or frieze, too, including the graceful festoons, central oval panel, and flanking frieze spots on the pilasters with their

nicely delineated figures, is a little masterpiece of
bas-relief in French putty.

The doorway of this room, like others in the house,
has considerable refined embellishment. Flat pilasters rise from the baseboard to the doorhead, beside
the casings, upon which hand-tooled reedings are
cut. The capital consists of a simple use of the
acanthus leaf taken from the Corinthian order.
Fruit-filled urns, garlands, and rosettes of applied
work ornament the broad frieze and pilasters of the
doorhead, which is virtually a complete entablature
including the favorite dentil course in its cornice
with reed cross-sections between the dentils, but
minus the tiny holes in each dentil of the main
cornice above, which are probably the marks of a
nail set purposely left unfilled. The door itself
pleases the eye with its well spaced and carefully
molded panels, and the brass drop handle corre-
sponds to those of the other principal rooms, but one
notices the substitution of modern butts for the old-
fashioned strap hinges of the west parlor.

On the floors above, the chambers architecturally
worthy of special mention correspond in treatment
to the rooms below, those in the earlier western
portion being Georgian and in the later eastern
portion Adam. Of them all, the east front and prin-

PLATE CVIII.—Detail of Embrasured Window, East Parlor, Pierce-Johonnot-Nichols House.

PLATE CIX.—Detail and Corner Section of East Parlor
Doorway, Pierce-Johonnot-Nichols House.

PLATE CX.—Detail of East Front Chamber Mantel, Pierce-Johonnot-
Nichols House; Corner Section of the same.

PLATE CXI.—East Front Chamber, Pierce-Johonnot-Nichols House; Architectural Treatment of Rear Wall.

cipal guest chamber excels. Reversing the usual order of projection, the chimney piece has been recessed slightly more than the width of the shelf between flanking closet doorways, the entire end of the room being architecturally treated in wood. The chimney piece itself seems to be a delightfully simplified reflection of the one below with engaged columns instead of pilasters to support the shelf. The reversed position of the reeded ovolo and dentil course in the cornice, the omission of the ovolo from the shelf, the absence of the frieze above and the pilasters at the side of the panel over the chimney breast, also the fluted band about the fireplace opening, constitute the chief differences. The mantelboard is typically Adam, with a central panel of vertical flutings and garlands and flower-filled urns of applied work at each side. In its very restraint and nice selection of simple ornament lies that charm which renders this one of the most admired mantels in New England.

As an example of the delightful architecture of Salem's prosperous days, this old house amply repays the critical study of students or prospective home builders, and it seems the more remarkable when one recalls that in those days all the smooth finish and moldings had to be made with hand planes, and all decoration cut out with chisels or applied with composition. It is especially notable for its chaste elegance, the delicacy of its carving, and the careful manner in which they are subordinated to the more important structural features; skilful balance is always maintained between plain surface and dainty decoration. These qualities are the fruit of McIntire's genius, his painstaking craftsmanship, his exhaustive study of the best architectural publications of his time, and his keen sense of harmony and proportion.

Plate CXII.—Detail of Porch and Façade, Assembly House.

PLATE CXIII.—The Assembly House, erected in 1782.

CHAPTER VIII

PUBLIC WORK

ALTHOUGH McIntire is known primarily as a designer of homes, his versatility led him on numerous occasions into the field of public work, where he acquitted himself with success and even renown. Virtually from the very outset of his career as an architect, and almost until its untimely close, he was engaged more or less regularly upon buildings of a public or semi-public character, for as his winning personality and frequent achievements in domestic design ever strengthened the esteem and admiration of his fellow citizens, they saw to it that he found opportunities to serve the town, the county, and even the nation.

As early as 1782 we find him designing Assembly Hall at Number 138 Federal Street, the assembly house of the Federals, political rivals of the Democrats whose headquarters were later established in Washington Hall, also designed by McIntire. At once this building took its place among the foremost social centers of the town and became the scene of many receptions, balls, banquets, and other functions. Here La Fayette dined during his first triumphal tour of America in 1784, and here also Washington danced at a ball given in his honor in 1789. In 1795 the building was remodeled for dwelling purposes, Judge Samuel Putnam being among those who occupied it.

This hip-roofed and decked house bespeaks attention chiefly for the elaboration of its flat-boarded façade with Ionic pilasters on the second story under the pediment, within which a pleasing fanlight is located to admit light to the attic. Here, as elsewhere in McIntire's work, it will be noticed that the order has been employed with considerable license, particularly in the capitals. The porch claims special notice because of its festoons, ornamental scroll corners, and heavy grape frieze — vine, leaves, and fruit being life-size and carved out of wood in a masterly manner.

Of McIntire's second venture in this larger field the *Massachusetts Magazine* for March, 1790, states:

"The Court Houſe in Salem, is a large, elegant building, and ſtands towards the end of a handſome ſpacious street. On the lower floor, on the eaſtern

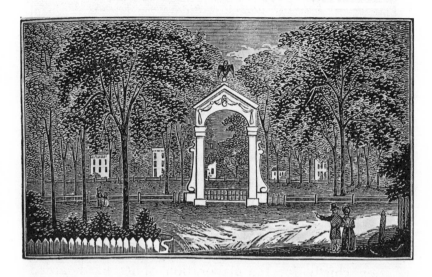

Plate CXIV.—Western Gateway, Washington Square, erected in 1805, from a Woodcut in "Felt's Annals of Salem"; St. Peter's Episcopal Church, razed in 1833, and the Western Gate in the distance, from an old painting.

PLATE CXV.—The Courthouse of 1785, from an old painting at the
Essex Institute; also, from an engraving in the *Massachusetts
Magazine*.

fide, is a range of offices, large and convenient; one
of which is occupied by the Clerk of the Court of
Common Pleas for the county of Effex; in which are
kept all the records of that court: The other two are
ufed as offices, for the Selectmen and Affeffors of
the town of Salem. The remainder of the lower
ftory is a fine capacious area, for walking &c.

"The fecond ftory is compofed of a large court
hall, with feats on every fide, for the Judges, officers
of the court, and for the auditors — faid to be the
best conftructed room, for the holding of courts, of
any in the Commonwealth, and perhaps is not ex-
ceeded by any in the United States. In the ceiling
is a handfome ventilator. Back of the Judges' feat
is a Venetian window, highly finished in the Ionick
order; which affords a beautiful profpect of a fine
river, extenfive well cultivated fields and groves;
in addition to which, the paffing and repaffing of vef-
fels continually, in the river, makes a pleafing
variety. There is alfo on this floor a convenient
lobby for Jurors &c. This houfe was begun in 1785,
and completed in 1786, at the joint expenfe of the
county of Effex and town of Salem. The plan of it
was defigned by the ingenious Mr. Samuel M'Intire
and executed by that able architect, Mr. Daniel
Bancroft, both of Salem."

Felt, in his "Annals of Salem", describes it still further:

"It was planned by Samuel McIntire, and built under the direction of Daniel Bancroft, two ingenious architects. It was two stories high, 62 feet long, and 36⅔ feet broad. It was finished in 1786. Its cost was $7,145, paid, one moiety by the town and the other by the county. Its walls were of brick and its roof surmounted by a cupola. On the front or southern end of it, was a balustrade, opening into the second story, supported by a row of Tuscan pillars. Under the balustrade were wide stone steps, which could accommodate a large number of persons and which led into a door of the lower hall. On the east side of this hall were several offices and the rest was left open for public assemblies and the exercise of military companies. The part thus occupied for the last purposes, was too often appropriated by unruly boys to their boisterous sports and destructive propensities, until large *bulls* of authority sounded in their ears and drove them from the premises."

Examination of the records at City Hall would seem to indicate that the total cost of the Courthouse was much greater than Felt states. One additional appropriation of six thousand dollars and another of

Plate CXVI.—Interior of Washington Hall, erected in 1792.

PLATE CXVII.—Mantel from the Old Registry of Deeds Building, erected in 1807.

three thousand dollars are certain, and surely such
a brick building must have cost at least twenty thousand dollars.

This much admired work of McIntire, erected in
1785, was located in the middle of Washington Street,
north end, nearly opposite the Tabernacle Church,
as shown by several old steel engravings and a contemporary oil painting preserved at the Essex Institute. There it stood until 1839, when the building of the railroad tunnel beneath necessitated its
removal, and the porch columns were removed to
the Chase house on Federal Street. It was from
the balcony over this porch that Washington was
presented to the townspeople on the occasion of his
visit October 29, 1789. Here he stood bowing
his acknowledgments while odes were sung and
the populace shouted itself hoarse. Meanwhile
McIntire, seated at a window near by, studied the
features of the first president minutely, and made
a sketch which formed the basis for his famous
profile bas-relief, thirty-eight by fifty-six inches
and executed in wood, which for years adorned the
architectural gateway at the western entrance of the
Common and now hangs in the Essex Institute.

In 1792 Washington Hall, Number 101 Washington
Street, was erected after plans by McIntire, and as

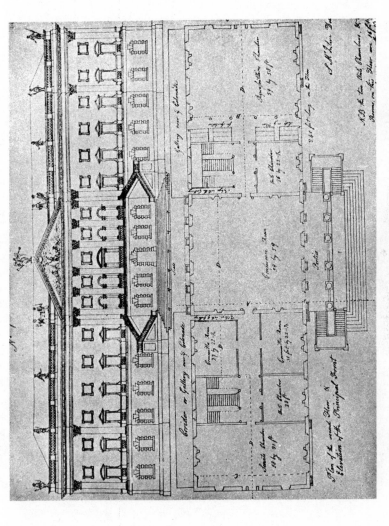

PLATE. CXVIII.—Principal Elevation and Second Floor Plan, Proposed National Capitol.

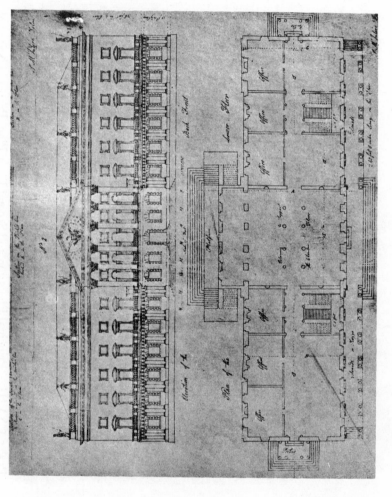

PLATE CXIX.—Rear Elevation and First Floor Plan, Proposed National
Capitol.

intimate knowledge of the Renaissance in Italy, France, and England, and the combined use of the Corinthian and Doric orders on the rear elevation again emphasizing McIntire's characteristic disregard of traditional restraint. Although eminently pleasing, the scheme did not possess the grandeur or the novelty of that submitted by William Thornton, superintendent of the Patent Office, which was finally chosen and considerably modified and altered during the course of construction by B. H. Latrobe and Charles Bulfinch who in turn succeeded to the post of Architect of the Capitol after Thornton's death in 1827.

McIntire's name will ever be inseparably associated with the Common, a tract of about eight acres, formerly the training field of Salem and since 1802 known as Washington Square. In 1801, Elias Haskett Derby, then a colonel in the militia, raised a fund of about twenty-five hundred dollars to which he contributed largely for grading, planting trees, and otherwise improving it, and in 1805 further contributions were made by individuals and the town to surround the entire field by a wooden fence with four ornamental gateways. The principal ones at the eastern and western entrances are described by Felt, in his "Annals of Salem", as follows:

The Wood-Carver of Salem

"Being designed, arched, and ornamented by Mr. Samuel McIntire, a noted architect, they do much honor to his taste."

The accompanying woodcut, also reproduced from the same volume, gives a general idea of its quaint appearance. Surmounted by one of McIntire's best sculptures in wood — a gilded eagle — the face of the arch below bore the famous profile medallion of Washington already referred to — a fitting adornment in view of the fact that in naming the field Washington Square it had been dedicated to the memory of the "father of his country." In 1850 the wooden boundaries were replaced by the present iron fence, and the eagle over the gateway was transferred to the façade of the City Hall, where it remains to this day a conspicuous reminder of the past, finely executed and much admired by all who examine it critically. One or both of the unidentified carvings now in the possession of the Essex Institute and shown in Plate 119 according to final arrangement were probably features of the eastern gateway of Washington Square.

Although not a McIntire design, the old Customhouse at Number 6 Central Street is better remembered for his sculptured eagle placed over the doorway in 1805 than for the building itself. Since the

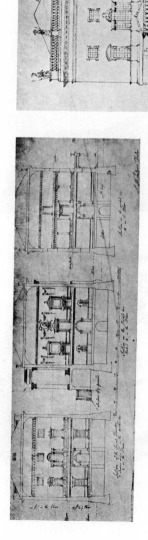

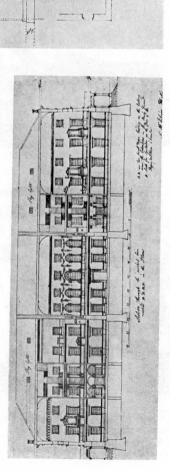

PLATE CXX.—Interior Sectional Plan, at three points, Proposed National Capitol; Exterior End Elevation; Interior Sectional Plan.

PLATE CXXI.—Hand carved Gilt Eagle on the City Hall, 1805;
A Carving at the Essex Institute; Sculptured Eagle formerly over
the Old Custom House Door, 1805; another Carving at the Essex
Institute.

present Custom-house was erected in 1818, the older
building has been devoted to miscellaneous private
business ¦purposes, and the eagle was finally transferred to the Essex Institute for safe-keeping. Of
life size, and hand tooled in full relief with superlative nicety, this piece of the authenticated personal
carving of McIntire may confidently be regarded
as one of his greatest achievements in sculpture.
Along with it may be classed his profile of Washington, the eagle on City Hall, and the figure on the roof
of the Derby summerhouse. Two other important examples of a similar character but of unknown
original location form part of the Essex Institute
collection and deserve high praise.

When called upon to do so in 1804, McIntire did
not hesitate to essay his skill in the very different
and difficult art of church design. Indeed, a few
writers of the present day, eager to enlarge the list
of his accomplishments, have hazarded the proba-
bility that he may have been responsible for the
beautiful steeple of the Park Street Church, Boston,
but no authentic record has ever been found to prove
it, and for years it has been known that the church
proper was designed by Peter Banner, an English
architect, and that the Ionic and Corinthian capitals
of the steeple were the work of Solomon Willard,

the architect who superintended the construction of Bunker Hill Monument.

Certain it is, however, that McIntire designed the South Church, Orthodox Congregational, on the northeast corner of Cambridge and Chestnut Streets, Salem, which came as the result of a separation from the Tabernacle Church in 1774 under the leadership of Colonel Timothy Pickering. Until the edifice was erected, the new society occupied an assembly hall that stood on adjoining land, and in which many notable functions were held before the Revolution, among them a reception tendered to Governor Gage on the last King's Birthday celebrated in Massachusetts. When completed, the church was considered one of McIntire's greatest works. Its dimensions were sixty-six by eighty feet with a graceful spire after the Wren manner one hundred sixty-six feet high, and together with the land it cost $23,819.78. The following description of it by James Gallier, an architect, occurs in the *North American Review* for October, 1836:

"One of the best proportioned steeples in our country is at Salem, in Massachusetts; the work of a native artist. The whole church is the best specimen of architecture in that city, notwithstanding the various efforts which have been made since its

PLATE CXXII.—The Old South Church, Salem, erected in 1804.

PLATE CXXIII.—Hamilton Hall, erected in 1805; Detail of the Second Floor Windows and Sculptured Panels.

erection. We are not aware that it has any name; but the building will easily be recognized as the only church in Chestnut Street. The Ionic portico in front is uncommonly elegant, though simple and unpretending. Above this rises the steeple, to the height of nearly a hundred and fifty feet. Its principal merit is beauty of proportion, which is not equalled in any steeple, that we know of, in the United States."

This noble example of his versatility in design, under the very shadow of which McIntire lived, was generally speaking Ionic, with touches of Adam detail here and there except for the bell deck, where the cornice, frieze, and flat pilasters are pure Doric. It was from this bell deck that Captain Oliver Thayer watched the naval battle between the *Chesapeake* and the *Shannon*, June 1, 1813. Below, the base of the steeple, clapboarded like the building proper, has quoined corners after the manner of stonework. Within this steeple was housed an interesting piece of homemade mechanism said to have been constructed by a Beverly blacksmith, possibly Samuel Luscomb, who also made the clock for the East Church, of which Reverend William Bentley, the historian, was pastor for thirty-six years. The clock in the South Church had no face and was provided with works only for striking the hour. It was originally in the First Church at Essex and Washington Streets, then removed to the Old North Church on North Street in 1826, and finally to the South Church ten years later. An iron frame, a pendulum ten feet long, and weights consisting of wooden boxes filled with stones were among its curious parts.

A distinctive feature of the interior of the church was a large crystal chandelier imported in 1807. It had arms for thirty candles and is said to have cost one thousand dollars. For almost a century this edifice stood one of Salem's most picturesque landmarks until destroyed by fire in 1903. Several of the hand-carved urns from the steeple, fortunately rescued from the ruins, are now in the possession of the Essex Institute.

There also may be seen a fireplace and mantel taken from the Old Registry of Deeds Building, erected in 1807 on the corner of Broad and Summer Streets, which was razed when the State Normal School was built. The mantel is one of McIntire's simplest and best proportioned, and the public character of the building gave him an opportunity to employ one of his ever-popular eagles for the central panel of the mantelboard or frieze.

PLATE CXXIV.—Side View of Hamilton Hall.

PLATE CXXV.—Entrance Doors and Music Balcony, Hamilton Hall; one of the Side Walls.

In 1804 McIntire was also the architect of the Branch or Howard Street Church built on a lot of land in an open field back of Brown Street, Howard Street not having been laid out at that time. No photograph showing its exact appearance is known to exist, but Reverend C. C. Beaman, speaking before the Essex Institute in 1861, referred to it as "a spacious and handsome edifice", and it is on record that the total cost of the land and building was about fourteen thousand dollars. Seven master carpenters took separate parts of the work on contract, viz., William Doliver, Joseph Eveleth, Daniel Farrington, George H. Smith, Asa Flanders, Joseph Fogg, and Peter Frye. Shaw and Lovett, of Beverly, did the mason work. What better proof could there be that McIntire was an architect rather than a mere carpenter or wood-carver and worked in a manner similar to that of the architect of to-day?

After its dedication, February 6, 1805, this church continued for many years to be one of the important places of meeting in Salem. Here on August 23, 1813, Judge Joseph Story delivered his famous eulogy of Captain Lawrence and Lieutenant Ludlow of the *Chesapeake*, who were killed in that memorable engagement with the *Shannon*, already referred to, which was fought so near shore that many persons watched it from the highest hills in this vicinity. Finally, after many vicissitudes, the building was sold at public auction in 1867. The structure was taken down, and such of its material as was suitable was used in the construction of the First Methodist Meeting House on Railroad Avenue, Beverly. Mr. Peter Clark, of Beverly, who was on the building committee, states that the frame and boarding was used, but that new clapboards, shingles, and a new tower were necessary. A new first story was also added, so that to-day only that part with the high church windows and the roof retain the form and appearance of the original. Probably none of the exterior wood trim was retained, though some of the inside doors are the originals.

That remarkable statesman and economist, Alexander Hamilton, had many ardent admirers in Salem. Several prominent citizens counted him among their personal friends, and the townspeople had seen him in their midst in the pursuance of his military duties and felt that they knew him. And so in 1805, when the South Building Corporation, an association of wealthy men, decided to erect a building for assemblies on the southeast corner of Chestnut and Cambridge Streets opposite the South Church, they named it Hamilton Hall. Here La

PLATE CXXVI.—Fireplaces, Vaulted and Groined Ceiling, Hamilton Hall.

PLATE CXXVII.—Detail of Mantel, Hamilton Hall; Corner Section of Mantel.

Fayette dined with three hundred guests on August 31, 1824, during his second triumphal American tour, when he was presented with the sum of two hundred thousand dollars and a township of land by the government in recognition of his services to the nation during the Revolution. Here, likewise, Commodore William Bainbridge, commander of the famous frigate *Constitution* in succession to Captain Isaac Hull, also Timothy Pickering, a politician with a record of public service equalled by few Americans, were accorded the full measure of Salem hospitality; and indeed, ever since its erection, this building has remained the very heart of the social activities of Salem.

Exteriorly the structure boasts little adornment other than its purely utilitarian features. The entrance porch at one end has been so remodeled as to make it difficult to judge with certainty of its original appearance. The sides, however, remain unchanged, except that the brickwork has been painted, and are pierced on the second and principal floor by five Palladian windows of the simplest sort, somewhat recessed under a double arch of brick headers. A rectangular insert above each window displays one of McIntire's sculptures, that in the center being one of his well-known eagles, and the others being the festooned drapery which he sometimes used on a smaller scale on doorways and mantels.

Dignified simplicity characterizes the interior treatment of the hall, which consists of fluted pilasters in pairs at the corners resting on pedestals corresponding to the flat dado with molded base and surbase and supporting a heavy cornice entirely of planed moldings. Above, the ceiling is groined, producing a pleasing effect over the two fireplaces at one end of the hall with their mantels of corresponding simplicity, though distinctive in the substitution of a hand-tooled, vertical fluted molding for the usual dentil course, as well as for the vertical reeded ovolo beneath it. A music balcony with handsome balustrade graces the opposite end of the hall over the double entrance doors, and in the cornice one notices again the double denticulated Grecian band so familiar to every student of McIntire's work. The single doors, both in arrangement and spacing of their stiles, rails, and molded panels, represent this notable architectural period at its best.

INDEX

INDEX

A

ACANTHUS FLOWER, 100
Acanthus-leaf, on Peabody-Silsbee house, 50; at "Oak Hill", 77; applied to the cymatium of the mantel-shelf, 100; in Cook-Oliver house, 115; in Pierce-Johonnot-Nichols house, 130
Adam, the Brothers, influence on McIntire, 25, 43, 79, 87, 93, 99, 120, 123, 127, 143; furniture, 65; urns, 75, 94; mantel, 88; festoons, florets, sculptured panel, 94; mirror, 97; garlands, 98, 109; lintel, 125; balance, 128; chambers in manner of, 130; mantelboard, 131
Adaptation, Salem architecture shows clever, 9, 27; Colonial style bends itself to, 14, 15; McIntire's faculty for, 44, 104, 110, 121; Colonial, 75
Almshouse, Salem, 30
American Antiquarian Society, 18
American antiquities, 6
American architecture, 5, 12, 14, 19
American style, foundations for, 14; will probably always be Colonial, 14
Amsterdam, 103
Andirons, 87, 101
"Annals of Salem", 19, 31, 103, 136, 139

Applied work, 25, 26, 68, 70, 92; at "Oak Hill", 75, 76, 77, 79, 100, 101; in Pierce-Johonnot-Nichols house, 83; in Derby-Crowninshield-Rogers house, 83, 94, 124, 129, 130, 131; in Lindall-Barnard-Andrews house, 87, 90; in Hosmer-Waters house, 88, 89; in David P. Waters house, 95; in "The Lindens", 98; in the Cook-Oliver house, 112, 113, 115
Arches, over gate, 60; of Pickman House, 62; ceiling of cupola, 64; of china closet doors, 74; elliptical, 80, 121; in Washington Square, 140; in Hamilton Hall, 147
Architects, Salem, their method of treating the classic orders, 10, 11; of Samuel McIntire's time and of the present day, 31, 32. *See* WOOD-CARVERS; JOINERS
Architecture, Salem. *See* SALEM
Architrave, casings, 9; in Peabody-Silsbee house, 51; in Pierce-Johonnot-Nichols house, 61; in Hosmer-Waters house, 88; in Peabody-Silsbee house, 89; bearing most of the ornament, 91; in David P. Waters house, 95, 97; in "The Lindens", 98; in Cook-Oliver house, 110, 112, 115
Assembly Hall, Salem, 133

Index

Association for the Relief of Aged and Destitute Women, 53
Atlantic, Derby's ship, 105

B

BAINBRIDGE, COMMODORE WILLIAM, 53, 147
Balcony, music, 148
Ball molding, 51
Balusters, 81, 83
Balustrades, 9, 31; porch, of Peabody-Silsbee house, 51; roof, of Dow house, 60; roof, on Pickman - Derby - Brookhouse estate, 63; in Hosmer-Waters house, 81; McIntire's, 83; in Cook-Oliver house, 109, 112; in Pierce-Johonnot-Nichols house, 121, 124; in Courthouse, 136; in Washington Hall, 138; in Hamilton Hall, 148
Bancroft, Daniel, 31, 135, 136
Bands, 56, 110, 116; fascia, 70; of guttæ, 90; of spheres, 91; of flutings, 96, 129; of reedings, 97
Banner, Peter, 141
Barnard, Rev. Thomas, 20, 87, 88
Barns, 60, 63
Base, of fence, 55, 108; of pilaster, 77; of wainscot, 112; dado with, 125, 148
Baseboard, 68, 69, 72, 77, 81, 130
Bas-relief, 92, 93, 94, 100, 130, 137
Bead and reel, 95, 126; and dentil, 124
Bead molding, 115
Beaded border, 75
Beaman, Rev. C. C., 31, 145
Becket's shipyard, 5
Bed-molding, 11, 87, 94; bears hand-tooling, 88; denticulated,

93; in Derby-Crowninshield-Rogers house, 96; in "The Lindens", 97
Belasco, David, 121
Belvedere, 5, 9; of Peabody-Silsbee house, 51; of Pierce-Johonnot-Nichols house, 121
Bentley, Rev. William, 18, 20, 29, 30, 143; extract from his diary on death of Samuel McIntire, 35, 36, 41; describes visit to Derby farm, 104; oration made by, 138
Beverly, Mass., 143, 146
Blinds, 95, 109, 111
Boston, Mass., 4, 71, 141
Bowditch family, 59
Box stairs, 83
Boys' club, 30
Brackets, scroll, 83
Bradstreet, Governor Simon, 59
Branch Meeting House, 31, 145
Brass, hardware, 54, 123; knobs, 78, 113; andirons and fire set, 87, 101; hob-grate, 116, 126; drop handles, 127, 130
Brick, 33
Broad Street, Salem, 144
Brookhouse, Robert, 53
Brown, Colonel William, 103
Bulfinch, Charles, 28, 30, 34, 139
Bunker Hill Monument, 142
Busts, 41
Butts, 130

C

CAMBRIDGE STREET, SALEM, 61, 142, 146
Capitals, Ionic, 49, 60; of Kimball house, 49; of the Peabody-Silsbee house, 50, 89, 91; in McIntire porch, 63; at "Oak Hill", 77, 79; in Hosmer-Waters house, 87; in Derby-

Index

Crowninshield-Rogers house, 95; in David P. Waters house, 97; in Pierce - Johonnot-Nichols house, 124, 128, 129, 130; in Assembly Hall, 134; in Park St. Church, Boston, 141

Capitol, the, at Washington, 31, 34, 138

Carlton, Rev. Michael, 53

Carving, equal to best sculpture, 25; in Peabody-Silsbee house, 51; on fireplaces, 85; for Lindall - Barnard - Andrews house, 87; delicacy of, in Pierce-Johonnot-Nichols house, 132; unidentified, 140

Casings of doors and windows, 9; molded after manner of architrave, 75; with groups of flutings, 76; molded pilasters as, 79; in Cook-Oliver house, 109, 110, 122; in Pierce-Johonnot-Nichols house, 122, 124, 128, 130

Castiglioni, Count, 62

Cavetto molding, 63

Ceiling, of Samuel McIntire's house, 22; of Pickman-Derby-Brookhouse cupola, 64; of Cook-Oliver house, 105, 113; groined, of Hamilton Hall, 148

Central Street, Salem, 140

Chambers, 69, 70, 76, 87, 89, 99, 100, 130, 131

Chandelier, 144

Charter Street Burial Ground, Salem, 39

Chase house, 137

Chesapeake, the, 143, 145

Chestnut Street, Salem, 142, 143

Chimney breast, 99, 129, 131

Chimney pieces, 6, 76; McIntire's, 29, 125; considered in detail, 85-101; of Pierce-

Johonnot-Nichols house, 128, 129, 131

China closets, 74

Chippendale, 65, 123

Chisels, 10, 42, 125, 132

Churches, 141-145

City Hall, Salem, 30, 136, 140, 141

Civil War, the, 13

Clapboards, 109, 143

Clark, Peter, 146.

Classic detail, 7, 9, 27; in Peabody-Silsbee house, 50; in Derby - Crowninshield - Rogers house, 73; in Pierce-Johonnot-Nichols house, 126

Classic orders, 8, 11, 69, 91, 104

Clock, 81, 112; of South Church, 143

Cloutman, Joseph, 30

Codfish, 62

Colonial, scope of the word as applied to Salem architecture, 5, 6

Colonial period, 7; work, lightness and grace of, 9, 10; houses, 29, 44; motive, in doorways, 47; interiors, three classes of, 68; doorways, 51, 79; adaptations, 75; hall, 80; furniture, 89; rooms, 114

Colonial style, 5; square house, 8; principal theme in American architecture, 12; persistence of, 13, 16; will probably always be the American style, 14; grace, repose, and dignity of, 14; embraces expressions of Dutch, French, and English peoples in America, 14; the intrinsic merit of, 15; its adaptability to new uses and requirements, 15; not restricted in its possibilities,

Index

Index

Index

Dolliver, William, 145

Doorhead, 75, 76, 77, 127, 130

Doors, 9, 54; without glasswork, 47; with leaded side lights, 47; in Peabody-Silsbee house, 51; three panels wide, 57, 62; of Dow house, 60; leaded glass, 74; six-panel, 77; in Cook-Oliver house, 113; in Pierce - Johonnot - Nichols house, 120, 122, 125, 127, 130; in First Methodist Meeting House, Beverly, 146

Doorways, 9; Salem famed for, 6; McIntire's, 29, 33; the keynote of the façade, 46; character and individuality, 46; reflect character of those for whom they were built, 47; the welcoming, 48; of the Kimball house, 49; of house on Derby Street, 54; leaded glass and three-paneled door a feature of, 57; the Tucker-Rice, 58; of Dow house, 60; of Hosmer-Waters house, 61; of Clifford Crowninshield and Derby - Crowninshield - Rogers houses, 75, 76; at "Oak Hill", 78, 79, 80; of Cook-Oliver house, 110, 111, 114; of Pierce - Johonnot - Nichols house, 122, 124, 130, 131; of Hamilton Hall, 148.

Doric order, in Stearns house, 51; in house on Derby Street, 53, 54; in Pierce-Johonnot-Nichols house, 61, 96, 122; in Woman's Bureau, 90; in Stearns Building, 138; in plans for Capitol, 139; in South Church, 143

Dow house, Josiah, 33, 59

Downing, Emanuel, 58

Downing, George, 58

Downing College, Cambridge, 58

Downing Street, London, 58

Drawing-rooms, 70, 72, 77, 78, 99, 100, 127

Drop handles, 78, 127, 130

E

EAGLE, THE, Samuel McIntire fond of carving, 17, 18; on Pickman - Derby - Brookhouse estate, 63; shield with, 90; on Pierce-Johonnot-Nichols estate, 121; on the Common, 140; on old Custom-house, 140, 141; on mantel from Old Registry of Deeds Building, 144; in Hamilton Hall, 147

East Church, 18, 35, 143

East Indies, 3, 105

Eaves, 9, 51, 57, 110

Eden, Thomas, 47

Eden-Brown house, 47, 49

Egg and dart motive, 90

Egg and tongue motive, 73, 126

Elevations, 31, 139

Elliptical arches, 79, 80, 121

Ells, 33, 63, 109, 116

Embargo Act, 118

Embellishment, 8, 33, 49, 55, 80, 85, 121, 130

Embrasures, 73, 74, 92, 116, 127, 128

Enclosed porches, 47, 48, 60, 61, 62, 122

Endicott, William C., 53

Engaged columns, 99, 111, 131

England, 25, 89, 127, 139

Enrichment, 87, 88, 94

Index

Entablature, 9, 11; of Kimball house, 49; of Peabody-Silsbee house, 50; of Stearns house, 52; of Tucker-Rice house, 57; Corinthian, of Waters house, 62; at "Oak Hill", 75; in Lindall - Barnard - Andrews house, 87; in Cook-Oliver house, 108, 110, 111; in Pierce - Johonnot - Nichols house, 130

Entrances, 46, 48; of Dow house, 60; of Pierce-Johonnot-Nichols house, 121

Essex Bank, the, 30

Essex County, 104, 135

Essex Institute, the Historical Collection of the, 29; McIntire's plans preserved at, 31, 103; tools preserved at, 42; Tucker-Rice doorway and porch at, 58; archway from Pickman house at, 62; cupola preserved at, 64; "Annals of Salem" at, 103; Captain Cook's portrait at, 106; fund being raised by, 120; pictures of Courthouse at, 137; balustrade at, 138; carvings at, 140; eagle at, 141; urns at, 144; speech of Beaman before, 145

Essex Register, The, 29; notice of death of Samuel McIntire in, 37

Essex Street, Salem, Benjamin Pickman house on, 48, 62; Peabody-Silsbee house on, 50; Stearns house on, 51; Tucker-Rice house on, 55; Gardner-White-Pingree house on, 56; Derby- Crowninshield - Rogers house on, 70, 72, 82; Lindall-Barnard-Andrews house on, 87

Eveleth, Joseph, 145

F

FAÇADES, flat-boarded, 8, 134; pilaster treatment of, 33, 34; doorway the keynote of, 46; three-story, 49; expanse of, 55; of Tucker-Rice house, 56; of Cook-Oliver house, 110

Facings, 86, 96, 97, 100

Fanlight, 47, 49; of Peabody-Silsbee house, 51; of house on Derby Street, 54; at "Oak Hill", 79; often used, 80; of Cook-Oliver house, 111; of Pierce - Johonnot - Nichols house, 121, 124; of Assembly Hall, 134

Farrington, Daniel, 145.

Fascia molding, 47, 49, 70

Federal, the word, 7

Federals, the, 133

Federal Street, Salem, 103, 133, 137

"Federal Street" hymn, 107, 115

Felt, the historian, 19, 136, 139

Fence, 51, 55, 57, 60, 108, 139

Fenceposts, 55, 60

Festoons, 48, 63, 64, 75, 83, 87; in Hosmer-Waters house, 88; in Adam manner, 94; in David P. Waters house, 95, 97; in Cook-Oliver house, 109, 113, 115; in Pierce-Johonnot-Nichols house, 125, 129; in Assembly Hall, 134; in Hamilton Hall, 148

Field, Elizabeth, 20, 22

Field, Samuel, 22

Fillets, 73, 89, 92, 95, 116, 129

Fireplace opening, 86; facings, 96, 97, 100; ogee moldings about, 126; fluted band about, 129, 131

Index

Fireplaces, 68, 74, 85, 86; in David P. Waters house, 97; in Cook-Oliver house, 116; in Pierce - Johonnot - Nichols house, 125; in Washington Hall, 138; in Hamilton Hall, 148

Fire sets, 87, 101

First Church, Salem, 144

First Methodist Meeting House, Beverly, 146

Flame motives, 108

Flanders, Asa, 145

Flemish tiles, 98

Florentine bent iron, 60

Florentine motives, 58

Florets, oval, 48, 63, 83, 95; circular or oval, 70; between garlands, 75; applied, 80; enrichment of frieze, 94; alternate, 100

Flower-pots, 75

Flowers, carved ornaments, 87, 91, 95, 100, 104

Flutes, 48, 70, 76, 77, 79; of Peabody-Silsbee house, 50; of pilasters of Dow house, 60; in Hosmer-Waters house, 87; in Crowninshield house, 96; in Pierce - Johonnot - Nichols house, 96, 121, 123, 124, 128, 131; in Cook-Oliver house, 108, 110, 113; in Hamilton Hall, 148

Fogg, Joseph, 145

Foreshortening, 56, 109, 121

France, 139

French Catholic Parish House, 59

French putty, 25, 76, 130

Fret, Grecian, 72, 77, 98, 100; interlacing fillet, 73, 92; in Pierce - Johonnot - Nichols house, 83, 123, 128, 129; lozenge, 116

Frieze, 9, 11; of Peabody-Silsbee house, 51, 89; of Pierce-Johonnot-Nichols house, 61, 75, 127–131; of Pickman house, 63; at "Oak Hill", 69, 73, 77, 79, 80, 99, 100; supplanting Grecian fret, 72; in Hosmer-Waters house, 87, 88; enrichment of, 87, 94; of Woman's Bureau, 90; advantages of beautifying mantel, 92; mantels with sculptured, 93; of Nathan Read house, 97; of David P. Waters house, 97; of Cook-Oliver house, 110, 111, 115; of Assembly Hall, 134; of South Church, 143

Frieze spots, 48, 98, 115, 129

Front Street, Salem, 103, 133, 137

Fruit, carved, 92, 98, 113

Fruit baskets, carved, 75, 77, 87, 95, 100, 130

Frye, Peter, 145

Furniture, white-painted interior setting for mahogany, 66, 67; the four famous types, 66; built-in, 73, 105, 138; collection of rare Colonial, 89; antique, 120

G

GABLE-ROOFS, 16, 21

Gage, General, 48, 142

Gallier, James, 147

Gambrel-roof type of architecture, 6, 8, 16, 17, 62

Gardens, 2; Derby, 103, 104; of Cook-Oliver estate, 112; of Pierce - Johonnot - Nichols estate, 118, 121

Gardner, Captain Joseph, 58

Index

Gardner - White - Pingree house, 33, 56

Garlands, 76, 130, 131; straight-hanging, 49, 75, 77, 88, 95, 108, 109; applied, 79; applied festooned, 83; Adam, 98; festooned, 115

Gateposts, 58, 102, 106, 108

Gates, 60, 108

Gateways, 122, 137, 139, 140

George, the, 59

Georgian style, 43, 120, 125, 130; windows, 60, 74, 109

Gibbons, Grinling, 43

Glass, Colonial, 111

Gouges, 10, 42, 129

Grand Turk, the, 105

Grape clusters, 75, 100

Grape-vines, 98

Grates, hob, 89, 116, 126

Gray, Lieutenant - Governor William, 53

Great Swamp Fight, 58, 59

Grecian bank, 148

Grecian Doric, 53, 54

Grecian fret, 70, 72, 77, 98, 100, 128

Greek revival, 7, 12

Greek temples, 44

Guttæ, of Peabody-Silsbee house, 51; of Pierce-Johonnot-Nichols house, 61; in the Woman's Bureau, 90

H

HALLS, at "Oak Hill", 69, 72, 80; in Cook-Oliver house, 70, 112–116; of Clifford Crowninshield house, 73; the Colonial, 80–82; in Pierce-Johonnot-Nichols house, 123, 124; in Courthouse, 136; of Hamilton Hall, 148

Hamilton, Alexander, 62, 146

Hamilton Hall, 146

Handrail, 82

Hardware, 54, 123, 127

Hardwood, 57, 67, 72

Harvard, John, 89

Headers, 147

Heppelwhite, 65

Heussler, George, 103, 104

Hinges, 127, 130

Hip roof, 9; Peabody-Silsbee house, 50; building of Association for the Relief of Aged and Destitute Women, 53; Clifford Crowninshield house, 55; Dow house, 59, 60; Cook-Oliver house, 109; Pierce-Johonnot-Nichols house, 121; Assembly Hall, 134

Hob grates, 89, 116, 126

Home for Aged Women, Salem, 52

Homer, Professor Eleazer B., 56

Hooper, Robert (known as "King"), 47

Horns of plenty, 95, 98, 101

Hosmer, Captain Joseph, 61

Hosmer-Waters house, 61, 81, 82, 87–89

Houses, reflect character of those for whom they were built, 47

Housewright, 17, 27, 32, 38, 107

Howard Street, Salem, 145

Howard Street Church, Salem, 147

Hull, Captain Isaac, 147

Hurley, John F., 59

I

INDIVIDUALITY, of doorways, 46, 122; of room, 125; lent by ends of frieze board, 127

Inserts, 91, 124, 147

Insurance company, 22

Index

Index

death, 20; marriage, 20, 22; first a carver, then designer, finally architect, 20; his home, 21, 22, 42; workshop, 22; mortgage, 22; music room, 22; musical instruments, 22, 40; office, 22, 42; inventory of effects, 22, 40, 41; Elias Haskett Derby's patronage, 23; as a designer, 24; recognized extent and limitations of his medium, 24; welcomed advent of stucco, 25; pleasing proportions of his work, 26; his plans, 26, 31, 34; work marked by refinement of detail and light and graceful effect, 26; called "The Architect of Salem", 30; buildings ascribed to, 31; his draftsmanship, 31; handwriting, 31; primarily a carver, 32; not contractor in modern sense, 32; brick adopted by, 33; depended on craftsmanship of two brothers, 26, 27; detractors, 27, 28; facts about, buried in the old records of Salem, 28; inspiration furnished by his work, 29; his place assured, 29; references to his talents as an architect, 29, 30; versatility, 33; his doorways, porches, etc., 33; his detail copied, 34; as a musician, 35, 37, 38, 40; death, 30; extract from Rev. William Bentley's diary on death, 35, 36; funeral, 36, 37; notices of death in *The Salem Gazette* and *The Essex Register*, 36, 37; personality, 36, 37, 39, 40; tribute to, in *The Salem Gazette*, 37–39; burial, 39;

gravestone, 29, 39; died intestate, 40; notice of sale of articles from estate, 40, 41; circumstances at time of death, 42; estate, 42; tools, 42; was not provincial, 43; appreciation of the man and his work, 43, 44; innovations of, 44, 50, 51, 63, 90, 91, 96–98, 126; imporant rôle of, 45; last work, 56

McIntire, Samuel F., 27, 31, 32, 40, 41

McIntire, Sarah (Ruck), 17, 20, 40

McIntire, family, influence of, upon the architecture of Salem, 30, 31

Mahogany, 65, 66, 82

Maine, 15

Mansions, of Revolutionary times, 7; bespeak earnest study, 11; of New England seacoast towns, 50, 67; square, three-story brick, 52; enclosed porch, feature of, 60; of 1750, 81

Mantelboard, 129, 131, 144

Mantels, of house at No. 31, Summer Street, 21; detailed consideration of, 85–101; in Cook-Oliver house, 114–116; in Pierce-Johonnot-Nichols house, 131; from Old Registry of Deeds Building, 144; in Hamilton Hall, 148

Mantel shelf, in Hosmer-Waters house, 87; in Woman's Bureau, 90, 91; in Home for Aged Women, 92; in David P. Waters house, 94; in Clifford Crowninshield house, 95; none in house of 1750, 96

Index

Index

Index

Reeds, of pilasters, 63, 89, 95, 97, 129; hand-carved, 70, 76, 130; band of vertical, 72; below the cyma recta, 73; frieze motive of, 80; in architrave, 92; twist-drill, 94; ovolo molding, 99; groups, 100, 128; symphony of vertical, 101; wainscot, 112; casings, 113; colonnettes, 115; central panel, 125; ovolo, 131, 148
Registry of Deeds Building, Old, Salem, 144
Renaissance, the, 4, 8, 11, 14, 44, 45, 139
Revere, Paul, 2
Revolution, the, 3, 7, 74, 103, 142, 147
Robinson, John, 63
Rogers, John, 64
Rogers, Mrs. J. C., 69, 71
Rogers, Richard S., 71
Roman Doric, 51, 111
Roman palaces, 44
Roofs, flat, 9, 61; hip, 9, 50, 53, 55, 59, 109, 121, 134; McIntire's, 33; balustraded, 56, 60, 63; figures on, 104, 105
Rope moldings, 10, 73, 83, 87, 89, 90
Rosettes, 51, 95, 125, 128, 129, 130
Rosewood, 65
Run (stairway), 112, 124

S

Salem, Mass., boasts well-preserved residential section, 1, 2, 4, 5; perfect condition of woodwork in houses of, 1; old houses of, recall the past, 2; next to Plymouth, the oldest settlement in Massachusetts, 2; merchants of, 2, 4; at the time of the Revolution, 2, 3; ships and shipbuilding of, 3; center of commerce and refinement after the Revolution, 3; chief port of entry, 3, 4; ships and tonnage of, in 1807, 4; Custom-house of, 4, 59, 140, 141; now lives in the glory of its past, 4, 5; the architectural center of New England for Colonial style, 5; a storehouse of American antiquities, 6; architecture of, embraces four dissimilar types, 6; scope of the word *Colonial* as applied to the architecture of, 6, 7; the square Colonial town house of, 8; modification of classic orders, 8, 9; characteristics of its architecture, 10, 11; everything of consequence in, is Colonial, 16; absence of monotony in architecture of, 16; during the early years of Samuel McIntire, 20, 21; home of Samuel McIntire in, 21, 22; houses at Nos. 70 and 90 Washington Street in, 22, 23; best carving of Samuel McIntire's time was done in, 23, 24; architecture of, stands as monument to Samuel McIntire, 28, 29; buildings designed by Bulfinch in, 30; Samuel McIntire's activities confined to old township of, 33; architecture of, from 1782 to 1811, 44; doorways of, have an atmosphere of their own, 47; porches of, possess charm and distinction, 48; charm of architecture of, 84; superiority of architecture of, 124

Index

Index